MOUNT PEACOCK

OR

PROGRESS IN PROVENCE

T0382317

THE HALT OF HILARION

MOUNT PEACOCK

OR

Progress in Provence

by

MARIE MAURON

Translated by

F. L. LUCAS

*"J'aime les paysans; ils ne sont pas assez
savants pour raisonner de travers."*

MONTESQUIEU

CAMBRIDGE

AT THE UNIVERSITY PRESS

1934

CONTENTS

CAMBRIDGE
UNIVERSITY PRESS

University Printing House, Cambridge CB2 8BS, United Kingdom

Published in the United States of America by Cambridge University Press, New York

Cambridge University Press is part of the University of Cambridge.

It furthers the University's mission by disseminating knowledge in the pursuit of
education, learning and research at the highest international levels of excellence.

www.cambridge.org
Information on this title: www.cambridge.org/9781107647183

© Cambridge University Press 1934

First published 1934
First paperback edition 2014

A catalogue record for this publication is available from the British Library

ISBN 978-1-107-64718-3 Paperback

INTRODUCTION

"L'esprit français est comme le vin français; il ne rend les gens ni brutaux ni méchants ni tristes."   TAINE

The English traveller bound for Cannes or Monte Carlo or India, as his *Rapide* thunders through Tarascon, remembers perhaps for a moment the illustrious Tartarin; glances, it may be, across the bushy green islands of the Rhone towards towered Beaucaire, where once Aucassin loved the white Nicolette; but never notices the grotesque little train that stands snuffling at his feet below the proud viaduct of the P.L.M.—ready at its own good leisure to clatter down its branch-line into the quiet heart of Provence, where the monuments of the Roman still stand beneath those bleached Alpilles which in days still older the Greek settlers of Marseilles must have found so like the limestone hills of home. That heart of Provence this book reveals.

Such is its first, its most direct appeal—the human comedy of lives still close to the simple strength of the soil in a land that still remembers the robust realism of the Latin and the pagan gaiety of Greece, still hides amid its grey olives the wisdom of Athene, still hears the lurking laugh of Pan in the pine-shadows of its thyme-clad hills; that still remembers also, a little bitterly, how even in the Middle Ages, when the Popes seemed to have succeeded in using the keys of St Peter to turn the lock upon the human mind itself and Kings grew pale before

Innocent III, this Midi still dared to live and think in its own way, while its troubadours sang the European lyric back to its second birth; until the Church let loose upon Provence from the greyer, harsher North that so-called Albigensian "Crusade", which slew on so stoutly in the simple faith that "God would know his own". Yet the Midi, though conquered, was not crushed. "Such a spirit of equality", writes Michelet of *cette poétique Provence*, "is nothing surprising in this land of little republics, in the midst of Greek cities and Roman municipalities. Even its countryside has never felt the weight of serfdom, like the rest of France." And to illustrate the persistence of that spirit he cites the Provençal admiral, "Paul the Cabin-boy", as to the end of his life he was called; who came into the world in a storm at sea, rose to the height of entertaining Louis XIV in person on his ship, yet died bequeathing his wealth to the poor and his dust to be laid with theirs. And in the century that followed, as English readers will recall, it was here "on the road betwixt Nismes and Lunel" that the Rev. Laurence Sterne footed it so gaily with his Nannette to "the Gascoigne roundelay—

> Viva la Joia,
> Fidon la Tristessa".

To this day Provence remains democratic—more than any country I have ever seen—with little sign of wealth or poverty; and with poetry, it still seemed, everywhere. I shall never forget meeting a certain elderly peasant-poet, "le Sauvage", with the face of an old Faun, sun-burnt deep terra-cotta, and the twinkling eye of a

Silenus. Summonsed for riding without a bell, he had turned his bicycle into a perfect belfry, jangling with some thirty odd; summonsed for riding without a light, he had saluted the local gendarme at their next meeting with a discharge of rockets from his handlebars; and the previous evening, when his fire refused to burn, he had exorcised it with complete success, he told us, by composing a sardonic poem to the effect that nothing else mattered, now that France had Alsace-Lorraine. Nor can I forget the more tragic figure described in the pages of a letter from the authoress of this book (and it pleases me even in an introduction to her work, which so little needs any, to be able to use her own words, even translated, rather than mine)—"Yesterday I saw an old woman who gave me a rare lesson—the Buddha himself pales beside her. Shall I tell you? Imagine that it's fine, that spring has really come, and that I am telling you this under the pines of Angiranny. She is eighty, this old woman, probably more; and lives alone in the very *mas**
where I was born—lovely it was once, though squalid now. She is blind and (I gather) a frightful cancer is slowly eating away her ghastly face. People take flight at her approach; the shopkeepers refuse to serve her and drive her away. Her five or six children, all peasants comfortably married, will not take her in, or even send her to the hospital, for fear of having to pay. Nobody will bother to find out if she eats, or what she eats, or whether she's warm or cold. After months of seclusion (this winter has been so long), she has emerged from her

* *Mas*, Provençal for "house", "farmhouse". (Cf. *maison*.)

hovel—an appalling sight, a groping bundle of rags and holes and grey wisps of hair straggling from under an unspeakable cap; her face eaten, her hands black and scaled like the back of an old chimney. It has been suggested to her that she might wash; she answers with a laugh (nothing so sinister as that laugh of hers) that washing is affected—showy—mere *coquetterie*. And what do you think she does, this leper and hermit, on her walks or in her cell? She composes verses! She asserts that in the ennui (merely the ennui!) of her existence she asked of God some distraction for her loneliness—and discovered in herself a gift of putting into rhyme stories, or reflections, or songs. They say she finds it a very adequate compensation; and when I tried to picture the bitterness of such an end to life, amid the ingratitude of her family (she who was such an affectionate soul that in her working days as a peasant she used to take out into the fields, with her six children, even her goats and her rabbits and her hens, so that they shouldn't feel bored, shut up in the darkness of the closed farmhouse), coupled with this terrible disease and her poverty and loneliness, her blindness and want—then they told me that, singing alone by her fireless hearth, she felt very happy and only asked to go on living; for poetry is a consolation for all things. I must own that I am so weak as to flinch from the sight of her—that, there by the roadside, I held my breath so that she should go by without suspecting my presence—that the bare idea of setting foot in her *mas*, or speaking to her, of facing her dead eyes and the scar upon that sinister countenance, wrings

my nerves. She is nothing to me; and her *mas*, though
I was born there, is nothing to me either now; but perhaps the sound of a human voice, one that she used to
know well, would bring into that ghastly life some respite and relief. Perhaps, too, there would be a lasting
lesson in such a sight, and even her poetry, which I
imagine to be so bad, might have some meaning—simply
in a human sense; for, as the poet puts it,

> qui chante
> Son mal enchante.

But why say all this, when I know I shall never have the
courage to take a step or say a word; when I stopped
dead by the roadside at the sight of that living ruin
coming towards me? I've known before now shepherds,
or others as poor and lonely, who yet found enchant-
ment in their own crude verses—if I told people, they
would only cry out that I was being lyrical and exag-
gerated; but I had never guessed that in a brain so simple,
in one who can't read, or write, or even count upon her
fingers, verse and song could have such a price and such
a power".

This has been a long quotation; but my readers will
not regret that. I have quoted it here both as an example
almost past belief of the consoling magic of the imagination, which may well stand on the threshold of a book
so full of it, and because, as a piece of Provençal por-
traiture, I feel that this tragic old woman deserves her
place beside the equally vivid characters of comedy that
follow—a comedy whose gracious laughter does not

forget, as it dies away—(it is enough to turn to the tale of "The Black Dog")—the underlying pitilessness of life. These figures of Mont-Paon—the unworldly old Liffran whose gentle stubbornness will not desert his sheep to go and claim the property he has inherited; the scapegrace Pascal who reels laughing into a Board Meeting, straight from dining for a wager off two hundred and eighty-three snails; Hilarion, the indulgent dictator of the asthmatic little train; or the Machiavellian Théophile, who contrives to combine the trade of quack healer and exorcist with the impassioned leadership of the Party of "Progress"—these rustics have the vitality, without the demoniac bestiality, of the peasant faces in a Russian film. They are (in the original) as racy of tongue as Synge's Irish, without the Irish touch of cold cruelty; as vigorous as the homely Scots of Sir Walter, without their Covenanting dourness; as human, as kindly, and as "Far from the Madding Crowd", as the natives of Hardy's Wessex, without the haunting melancholy of the Saxon. There are even moments when these Provençals may call up the Cotswold figures of a yet greater hand; at the military inspection of the motley horses of Mont-Paon there rises for an instant the stalwart spectre of a certain Sir John Falstaff, reviewing his village rabble of recruits; arm in arm with the portentous Théophile might stalk that Attic intellectual, Journeyman Bottom, or the constabular dignity of Dogberry. Though Théophile, indeed, recalls more clearly that other provincial oracle, politician, and journalist, Monsieur Homais, seen through a kindlier, less biting atmosphere than chills

Flaubert's Normandy. For the essential quality of this Provençal commune is that amid its most solemn and official formalities humanity is perpetually breaking in; until some sudden gust of laughter sends the last shreds of torn red tape blowing and bounding out of sight among the olive-trees.

"Or, l'âme aussi est un papillon."

Humour so good needs no explaining. There is no call to dwell on the comedy of these scenes whose gay satire never grows bitter with the tiniest touch of gall, though deepened at moments by a melancholy that seems, with quiet afterthought, to brood on the mystery of all laughter. But they possess also a further, more general interest both for the English reader and for the humanist of every race.

For, first, it is on the mutual understanding of France and England, the last two great peoples still left free in Europe, that may well depend the future both of Europe itself and of civilization. And for real sympathy and understanding even a little book like this may, I feel, do more than whole shelves groaning with treatises, whole columns of political oratory.

Secondly, throughout the modern world the two great enemies of the human spirit are, I believe, mechanism and mob-mindedness—the tyranny of the Machine and the tyranny of the Mass—the Americo-Russian mania for the Juggernaut of mere bigness and brute horse-power, and the Nazi-Fascist-Communist adoration of a mythic Moloch called the State. But this French Midi remains still incorrigibly individual—

simple, sane, human—the soil that bred Montaigne and Montesquieu. It can still laugh at the bureaucrat—"le maire et Montaigne ont tousiours esté deux"; it can still view the machine with a sense of proportion, as a servant, not a god.

Mont-Paon has no electric light. The burning question of those four street-lamps rends the Village Council with bitter debates between its Progressives and its Conservatives; and yet, in the final chapter, when it transpires that the price of this dazzling luxury, which so poor a commune cannot itself pay for, must be absorption in Arles, then, with a mingling of sublime and ridiculous, as one man Mont-Paon answers: "No!—we keep our freedom". The authoress, no doubt, was too intent on painting her picture to think overmuch of parables; and yet any painting of human nature as true as hers has its wider applications. The poor candles of Mont-Paon, like that of Latimer, become the symbol of another kind of illumination more lasting and more universal, though less visible—the freedom of the individual judgment from dictator and drill-sergeant, blue-book and bureaucrat.

Efficiency in the modern fashion is very well; electricity-grids can be an abundant blessing; but not at any price. In this Provençal hamlet is fought again in miniature the battle of the twentieth century. In Théophile with his mixture of mediaevalism and would-be modernity we may watch not only his inimitable self but also the village Hitler, the inglorious, though far from mute Mussolini, of a smaller world. And like their

Albigensian forbears in the Age of Monks, so these Provençals in the Age of Machines still cherish their own
doubts whether the earth's new masters are Creation's
final crown—even though the Machine, like the Monk,
for the moment prove too strong. And yet, after all,
to-day the Monk is gone; the bridge of Papal Avignon
is broken down; the spirit of humanity has in the end
proved stronger still. "France must be made banana-
minded"* cry the now familiar accents of the captain of
commerce from his American wilderness; but the retro-
grade inhabitants of Mont-Paon show no sign of becoming "banana-minded". They still eat the snails they
like; not the bananas they are adjured to like. They are
less startling than the noble savages on whom the
tortured soul of D. H. Lawrence set its forlorn hope.
But they have not taken a final leave of common sense.
And that is a certain advantage—even in these days.
They keep some of the wisdom of an older civilization,
forgotten by the herd-hysterias of Moscow and Detroit
—the wisdom of the Greek Diogenes who knew how
many things in life he did *not* want.

The patron-saint of neighbouring Tarascon is St
Martha; it is she that has latterly become the patron-saint
of our whole industrialized world—Our Lady of Labour,
"cumbered with much serving", bowed with material
cares, fretted with fugitive futilities. But in this work of
Marie Mauron lives a smiling, unlaboured reminder of
that sister of St Martha, who "chose the better part",

* This sublimity is culled from the admirable pages of
Paul Cohen-Portheim's *Discovery of Europe*.

and whom legend has likewise brought in her sister's company to Provence, to the little port of Les Saintes Maries de la Mer—famous in recent history for a Mayor more humorously reckless still than he of Mont-Paon. To me this little book with its gay, understanding laughter, its brave unembittered derision of the pompous and fanatical, its sense of the essential things in human life, its secret poetry, its grace, lies like a patch of evening sunlight amid the darkness that gathers round the horizons of a world gone mad.

GETTING IN TOUCH

Since yesterday a cart had been disgorging our packing-cases and dismembered furniture into the court, among the dismembered furniture and packing-cases of my predecessor, who was sadly behind his time-table. Never had the combined School and *Mairie* of Mont-Paon witnessed such a carnival. Departing tenants trying to depart, new arrivals struggling to arrive, were producing between them the most picturesque hullabaloo; and the Republic with her Cap of Liberty, enthroned on the façade of the building in an august serenity high above the hurly-burly of factions, was beginning to find plenty to amuse her. For more than forty years she had been waiting for something to happen; now came our removal to surpass all her expectations.

What endless trunks, mon dieu, what endless trunks!—trunks of wood, of fibre, of imitation fabric; trunks shaped like coffins, flayed of their pigskin, scraped, crazy, broken-cornered; trunks more modern, in nail-studded leather; even a cabin-trunk (saved from what shipwreck?—acquired by what freak of inheritance?); then piles of packing-cases, whose cracks disclosed books, medicine-bottles, a gridiron; heaps of sausage-shaped sacks, whence peeped here a boot, there the handle of an old syringe...

Leaving the horde of hirelings—movers-in and movers-out—bustling vainly to and fro, exchanging insults, and getting in each other's way, my Predecessor disappeared in despair into the open country; and I also withdrew, to deal with my new duties.

My notice of nomination was precise: "It will be your first step, by reporting to him personally, to get in touch with the Mayor; who will install you formally in your double and delicate functions of Schoolmistress and Mayor's Secretary. He will receive, if there is occasion, any complaints you may have to make. He will help you draw up the inventory, and will sign your report. You will realize what tact, what a sense of duty, what a spirit of conciliation..." I realized, I realized!

On the ill-paved road, that ancient Roman highway along which had swept once the Emperors of Arles, the sun of early afternoon sweltered perpendicularly down. But, like the village I had just left (five sun-blistered houses beside a main road), these drowsy fields with not a soul in sight did not seem to have much to offer "the double functionary" of the Republic. Not a child, not a householder! Plenty of cigalas chirped hidden in the dwarf-oaks. A thin thread of water lay sleeping at the bottom of the irrigation-canal. The road climbed and climbed. Before long the vines lost their foothold; the slope steepened; even the grass had died of drought between those dislocated flagstones; only the olives still mounted beside the dwindling track. Higher still, at the foot of the Alpilles (so blue, so white, while over them danced the hot summer air★) even the olives stopped dis-

★ "Danse la vieille"—"the old woman dances"—local expression for the shimmer of heat-mirage.

couraged, to throw their silvery necklace round the
craggy Grand-Paon—that chained "Peacock" whose tall
silhouette, with its tuft of black pines, dominated crouch-
ing village and sleepy plain.

No difficulty about finding the Mayor's house. It was
as described, "the only one on the right." But it proved
less easy to gain admittance. The moment I pushed open
the wooden gate, there rose a terror-stricken screaming of
guinea-fowl; geese came charging forward, snapping
their beaks; and a whole pack of dogs, choking with
frenzy, hurled themselves across my path. "Don't be
frightened!" cried the voice of a woman, invisible behind
a door covered with gauze to keep out the flies, "they bark
a lot, but they don't often bite." Then finally the master
of the house appeared, with half a white onion in his hand.
After dealing a few kicks to right and left, he was able to
lead me into a vast kitchen, very dark behind its closed
shutters. I found myself welcomed by the strong, friendly
grasp of the mistress's hands; she drew me to a seat at
table, where other hands thrust before me cream-cheese
with vinegar, olives, pimento-salad, honey, ham, fruit...
A strapping young fellow, setting down his glass of sour
wine, brushed the crumbs off his woollen pullover (Oh
tyranny of fashion, even here!) and introduced himself as
"Pascal," a neighbour, come out of good will (since time
pressed) to lend a shoulder at getting the grain into its
sacks.

"And the worst nuisance we have on our Municipal
Council," added the Mayor with a laugh.

"Nuisance or not," answered the young man gaily,

"you can't do without me. You've had bother enough, already, to find your ten freeholders among the hundred and twenty inhabitants of your commune. And if one of us dies, or moves, between now and the next elections, you'll have to go and borrow a Councillor from our neighbours."

"Oh, don't talk to me of elections!" sighed the Mayor. "We've three years yet; till then, I want to eat my bread in peace!"

The conversation grew lively. I had to explain who I was, where I came from, why and how I came to be here; and to make comparisons between the various posts I had held. From details of genealogy, topography, and economic geography the talk wandered to the harvest, the price of hiring threshing-machinery, the fickle promise of the vines. I gathered that the market for early vegetables had sagged, that the forwarding of fruit was going badly, that the blossom was failing to set owing to the early summer. At intervals I hazarded an allusion to the real purpose of my visit: but no one paid the slightest attention. It was too much a matter of course in their eyes that I should succeed their retiring schoolmaster. If only the storms that were besetting the Rhone Valley, would stop short of the Alpilles! "Our storms, you see, have a spirit of routine; once they start on a given track, devil take them if they'll change it! Nothing could be more chancy than living here at the foot of the mountains!" I tried to reach my objective by a new line of attack. In vain! It only led to a discussion of the misbehaviour of the wind, to execrations of the

"Tramontane" and, above all, of the "Narbonnais."
For, as you know—
                    De Narbonne,
            Ni bon vent, ni bonne personne!
Finally, by a cunning transition, I at last succeeded in
touching on the essential point of my errand—only to
find that the Mayor had himself only the haziest idea of
my "double and delicate functions." "Look here," said
he sententiously, "you just go your own way, without
fussing yourself; and remember, whatever happens, that
he that has must hold, and he that scolds, must scold, and
that any mortal thing may happen in this world." But I
was resolved to have the situation in black and white, and
not let him go rambling off again in the wake of Pascal, to
lose himself among olives with the black blight, or vines
attacked by mildew. "But we have to make the inventory together..."
    "What inventory?"
    "Why, of the furniture belonging to the school and
the municipality..."
    "Of the what...! Oh no, you're joking! There *is* no
furniture, my good lady. There may be in your schoolroom some worm-eaten tables, dating from the Flood.
We'll just make a bonfire of them, as soon as we can get
anything better; and meanwhile..."
    "Still we have to draw up a report..."
    "Report for whom? Why on earth?"
    "The report of my taking over, that I have to send in
to..."
    "But, really! What a notion! 'Report,' 'taking

over'...! No, look here, the whole thing's perfectly
simple. No need for all this red tape! Take over as best
suits you; the whole of that building is yours. The
Council Room will make a bedroom for you—nice and
airy! And if you have any wine, you just put it to mellow
in the prison—it's never been used for anything else.
There are shelves all round it, you'll find—very handy
it is."

"But when you summon your Council-meetings?"

"I? I never summon them! What would be the good
of doing that?"

"You don't...! But there *must* be an official meeting
once a month, with discussions of..."

"What! When I've anything to say to them, I just see
them at the café. But... you see, I never do have anything
to say to them."

"Then what reports do you send in to the Prefecture?"

"I?—to the Prefecture? None."

"But I'm sure—positive—that there *are* returns,
resolutions..."

"Oh well, if you're so sure, ask your predecessor what
he used to do. But I simply don't believe he ever sent in
all that stationery in his life. Anyway, you could always
just recopy his returns. You have a municipal rubber-
stamp; very well!—you stamp, you sign, you post off
whatever you like. You don't suppose, do you, that
anyone amuses himself by reading all those rigmaroles?"

"But in that case," I asked in despair, "what does the
Mayor's Secretary have to *do*?"

"Eh? Provided you get your salary every month, why

ask such a lot of questions? Don't keep yourself in a per-
petual fuss. Just take everything calmly and in due order
—like the dancers of Joncquières."*

"No, you *are* exaggerating," interrupted Pascal. "She
will have, now and then, various fussifications—a birth,
a death, conscripts called-up, or a couple married."

"Oh, *that's* nothing," laughed the Mayor. "The dead
just have to be buried. We've never tried pickling them.
And a marriage is simpler still. You bring the couple into
the schoolroom (being on the ground-floor, it serves as
the room-of-all-work); the happy pair sign the register;
and there you are! By the time they've got as far as that,
they ought to know their own minds, I should think? No
point in reading them out long rigmaroles—legal jargon
and 'whereases' and the rest of it. By the way, talking of
that, the widower from the Mas du Diable is remarrying
the day after to-morrow; well—"

"The day after to-morrow! But it's perfectly impossible. With two sets of furniture being moved now,
and straw all over the place."

"Straw's a sign of plenty, my good lady. Do you really
imagine straw or hay's going to upset them? They've
seen plenty more of it—never you worry! All that's of
no consequence—so set your mind at rest! Ah, one
moment, though—as you're wanting information, I'm

* The authoress explains: "Tradition tells that at Joncquières
the Mayor's daughter was so ugly that no one would ask her to
dance. So the Mayor made it a rule that all the girls should sit
ranged on a long bench and each cavalier take whoever fell to
him, when his turn came, without passing over any of them."

going to tell you the one drawback to your job—that is, when two lovers elope and send you to break the news to their parents."

"Oh no!"

"Eh, but you see!—we have no policeman, so you'll have to do it. Ah! I must say, *that's* not always a joke. For one father who greets you like a good fellow and offers you a drink, there are ten that put you through a regular catechism..."

"Or eject you on the toe of their boot," added Pascal.

"Yes, anything may happen. But it can't be helped. When you're at the head of a commune, in one way or another you have to pay for your position. It's the same with this drum here. *You* oughtn't to be bothered with it; still..."

"? ? ?"

"Yes, this drum. It's our fire-alarm. The commune's so poor that we've no church, no bell, and no fire-engine. So whenever in summer a row of cypresses catches fire, or a house, or a corn-stack, men have to be got together to make a chain of buckets. So we've invented this alarm-drum. Oh, to be sure, it's not devilish efficient; but we make it do. You'll see for yourself—not a difficult instrument, they say, to play. Anyway—think you can manage it?"

"And what else?"

"That's all. Except for the posters—naturally they're your affair. In winter we hardly get any; a few circuses in the neighbourhood, a distraint, or a sale of manure. It's in summer that the fun begins. Arles sends us notices of its fancy-dress fêtes; Beaucaire of its bull-fights; all the villages round have their patron-saint's days, their balls, their cinemas, their café-concerts; to say nothing of Government Loans, the Remounts Department, advertisements of fertilizers... The walls of the Mairie aren't big enough to take all the posters we get. So you have to stick them on the plane-trees along the road. I may say that this work—being, in its way, an extra—will bring you forty francs a year, cash down."

His wife, all ears, wagged at me an oracular forefinger: "Yes, wherever money comes from, it all helps to keep the pot boiling."

"Apart from this," added the Mayor casually, "you'll often have to write letters for somebody—or go and pay the taxes of somebody else—collect the shooting-licences of the careless ones—give advice here, play the peacemaker there... It's all part of your job. For instance, do try and have a talk with old Mother Canne and her daughter-in-law—they can't hit it off together. Toine mustn't be always taking his mother's side, as he does; or there may be trouble. And if a little brunette comes and asks for her papers so as to get married, you must just make her understand—"

"Oh, really!" cried Pascal. "A pretty Mairie, on my word, where girls have to be stopped from falling in love, and mothers-in-law from mounting high horses! Do you really suppose we've nothing more serious to do?"

At this the Mayor went purple. "What's not 'serious'? To wreck one's life—isn't that serious enough to suit you?

But any responsibility, of course, is a mere laughing-matter to you!"

"On the contrary, it's so little a laughing-matter that I'll tell you what I do think. We go on fussing about these fiddlesticks—it's time we changed our tune. *Yes!*—we *have* responsibilities to face! Yes!—we do want a Council-meeting! Yes!—we do want a discussion, a resolution, something done! What's the good of shutting your eyes to it? You *know* that there's a big question afoot —Electricity. You *know* that the village has made up its mind to have it—that there are certain pushing gentlemen who treat us as a lot of fossils and want to throw us out at the next election—"

"Oh, la, la! Let the fellow just try his hand at making up another list of candidates at Mont-Paon! I've already got everybody eligible!"

"—to throw us out and get the commune really going on the path of Progress!"

"Very well, then, they're welcome! I'll hand over to anyone that likes to try. Your Progress, my boy— oh, it makes my head ache! Look here! Haven't I done what you wanted—about this electricity, eh? Haven't I asked for a plan and estimate from the Rural Board of Works? Well, is it *my* fault if it's never come?"

"No. But all the same... Here we've been waiting months and months for it. And given that you've taken it on you to run things..."

"Oh, patience, patience! You just see—it'll come! You'll get it soon enough, your electricity—much good

it'll do you!—except break down, and set things on fire,
and attract lightning!"

"Pfffu..."

"Yes, certainly! The lightning runs along the wires.
Didn't you know that?"

Pascal choked with laughter. "You're superb. You're
all superb, the whole lot of you, with your scares. That's
why we beat all, here at Mont-Paon. No light, no post-
office, no telegrams, no washing-place, no drinking-
fountain—nothing, nothing at all! A railway-halt built
of reeds—of reeds, mark you! And an old wheelbarrow
of a train, that only stops for you if it happens to have time,
or likes the look of you. Not even a clock; we go by the
sun! By the sun!—in this twentieth century! I ask you!
Poor ninnies that we are! Every year we pay money into
the Treasury, instead of spending it on our own commune;
and go on living like so many ancient Romans! We can't
even put to rights the paved road they've left us, those old
Romans! *You* know that well enough, if anybody does
—since it's the only road to your place—*you* know whether
the stones in it are level or not! Every year you upset your
harvest-carts, and your grapes, on it!—and cut your
beasts' fetlocks!—and yet at the first whisper of repairs, you
behave just like your colleagues—put your hands to your
forehead—'No expenditure! Let's lie low! Economize!
Peace and quiet!' As if, at this time of day, one could live
on quiet—and economies!"

"Certainly *you* don't live on economy—still less, in
quiet—eh, you young devil! But the commune's poor.
You *can't* get away from that."

"Then borrow. No way of getting rich but borrow-
ing."

"Pretty notion! Ah, Pascal, if your poor father could
hear you!"

"Ask for Government-subsidies! Raise the rates!"

"Why not mortgage the whole commune while you're
about it? Is that what you call keeping pace with Progress?
You just think it over. I've lived longer. Take my word
for it. Up till now we've lived without fuss and without
debts..."

"And there's no reason, of course, why we shouldn't go
on telling the time by the sun, and do without letters,
bread, meat, medicine?—or go elsewhere for them, after
work-hours? The next village, eh, being only some two
hours away! And if I want to catch the train, what could
be simpler?—just light a bonfire on the track and yell like
a lunatic to make it stop! That's what we've always done
—so why not go on doing it a bit longer? Ah!—set of
slaves that we are! You old men, you go on looking back
to the past; but the past's past, and be damned to it! Let's
have a look at the present!"

By way of looking at the present, Pascal stretched out a
large arm, clad in green wool, across several centuries to
come.

But the Mayor only burst into a roar of laughter, and
filled our glasses with a golden liquid, fragrant of ripe
quince. "You're just like Théophile, when he lifts his
arms to heaven and cries—'Reactionaries! Fanatics!'
You wet your whistle, Pascal, it needs it, and don't go off
the deep end about things. You're young, you'll think

differently as you get older. We've all been like you in our
time; and just look at us now. A good pipe, a glass of
sémoustat,* and let the world rip! How do you like this?
—it has a sort of after-taste of sorb-apple. My poor father
always used to say that to make good *sémoustat*. . ."

When I had been duly enlightened on the best methods
of scenting *vin cuit,*† I tried to take my leave. It was not
very easy. Pascal, the Mayor, and his wife, all talking at
once with the wildest enthusiasm, were busy planning the
mock-serenade to follow the widower's wedding the
day after to-morrow. "Ah, it's great fun, once in a way,"
observed the Mayor, escorting me out through the midst
of his infuriated dogs. "You ought to get hold of a pail,
or a saucepan, and join in, if you like a good laugh! It
isn't every day one has the chance. As for the other
business, don't you bother your head at all. Take it or
leave it, jog along, and all's well that ends well!"

★   ★   ★

The Republic with her snub-nose was still looking down
from the façade of the Municipal Building at the picturesque bric-à-brac in the yard below. Perched on top
of a tottering bookcase, the furniture-remover's hirelings
were sharing in all brotherly love a stiff peg of anisette.
Not much progress had taken place in my absence; but
in the present state of affairs what signified a little more or

* Grape-juice mixed with alcohol to prevent it fermenting
and so keep it sweet.

† Grape-juice, boiled with quinces, but without alcohol, for
the same purpose.

less of chaos? The "double functionary of the Republic" began to feel she had plumbed the depths of human misery. And my predecessor, of course, was still nowhere to be seen! This was what they called "getting in touch!"

But who knows?—perhaps the Mairie itself could tell me more than the Mayor about this appalling question of my duties and responsibilities? Resolutely I made my way across piles of chairs, over heaps of broken glass, straw packing, boards bristling with nails, and gained the first floor—the official floor—of the Communal Building.

Black letters, more than half obliterated, marked the "Archive Room." Within it were some old clothes in rags, a coat-rack clinging to the wall by its last nail, and over by the windows, which would no longer shut, a tatter of yellowing lace; but nothing for an archivist or for any official eye. Then the "Council Room"—a couple of cupboards, a worm-eaten table on rickety trestles, and a blue carpet striped with red, a good deal the worse for clothes-moths and cigarette-ends. Against one wall stood two armchairs with broken seats; and on one of them a broken drum—the alarm-drum—my drum! On the other rested a decayed warming-pan. In one corner lay a flag riddled with holes, greenish-yellowish-rose in hue, with tarnished fringes—"that tricolour which has girdled the earth with the name, the glory, and the liberty of France." Next, some curtain-rods and curtains encircling a box of blue, grey, and red. May the Republic forgive me!—these were the electoral voting-room and polling-booth, where now reposed in peace the hairiest spiders in the whole *Département*. Finally behind the door—crown-

ing wonder of wonders!—a folding-bed, slept in the
night before; a pair of clogs; and some ancient pipes upon
a wooden stool. Such, in mid-removal, appeared the
Council Room—in reality, my Predecessor's Den.

Lightly the dust danced in the rays of the smiling sun—
settling, percolating, growing ingrained. Clothes-moths
with your fragile flight; death-watch beetles clicking in
the woodwork; pale mildews mouldering through these
ancient papers—what was I doing here, troubling your
quiet existence?

The cupboards proved as unused as the Mayor himself
to answering inquiries. The rusty keys stuck obstinately
in their locks. And when at last they yielded—what a
wealth of information! Inside, crinkled with age round
the drawing-pins that held them to the shelves, hung
cardboard labels, bearing in a fair round hand titles of a fine
precision—"Movements of Population"—"Military and
Naval Forces"—"Correspondence for the Year"—
"Drainage"—and (here beat the very heart of Mont-
Paon) "Births, Deaths, and Marriages."

Four black registers, bound in shagreen, held the whole
history of these, since the Year One of the Republic One
and Indivisible. First, through several pages, Citizen
Testanière kept his record in a large and gouty hand—"On
the 15th of Prairial, Year II, Jean-Pierre Espigue had by
his lawful wife an infant of the male sex... On the 10th
of Vendémiaire, Year IV, there were declared joined in
lawful matrimony..." But in the Year VI the pothooks
of Citizen Testanière faded away. For the whole of
Year VII, no entries. And at the opening of Year VIII a

new Registrar, whose illegible name was adorned with three concentric circles and two further flourishes in the shape of oak-leaves, recorded, as his first entry, the decease of the late Testanière. Then, through rare Births and still rarer Deaths, the black register jogged on; phrasing some recognition of illegitimate offspring under the Directory, pronouncing some legal separation under the Empire. Supported on the shaky pothooks of its signatures, it staggered its way through Revolutions and Terrors, through religious massacres and political deportations. Fire, that time-honoured destroyer of Archives, had spared this chronicle. But the rat's tooth and the worm's tunnel remain more formidable than Attila. The Testanière of the entries of Prairial, the Marquis de Mont-Paon of the Restoration, all its long line of Mayors, married couples, and deceased, were here slowly crumbling into one final dissolution beneath the dust and cigarette-ends of my predecessor.

"Movements of the Population" looked vitally important, in a commune of a hundred and twenty souls. It filled a whole shelf of bound volumes. But, alas, this mine of information proved to be really a complete set of the *Moniteur des Communes*. Here I learnt that in October 1852 the Prince-President Louis Napoléon Bonaparte, passing through Bordeaux in the course of his triumphal progress, proclaimed beneath a cloudless sky, "with a frankness as far removed from arrogance as from false modesty, that never had nation testified with more directness, spontaneity, or unanimity, its determination to rid itself of anxieties for the future by concentrating in a single hand an authority beloved throughout the country. (Wild enthusiasm and applause)... For the people recognized their debt of gratitude to him who had saved the ship of state by the mere act of unfurling the flag of France! (Loud and prolonged applause—shouts of *Vive l'Empereur!*)" At Toulouse the sunshine was no less dazzling, the enthusiasm no less indescribable—"Long live the Saviour of our Country!" As for the ecstasies of Agen...no pen could hope to cope with the ecstasies of Agen! But what superb weather they did have! What a plum-crop there must have been at Agen in that year 1852! As for what occurred at Auch, *that* we shall never know. Those leaves of the *Moniteur* were not even cut. I felt it beyond me to violate its Bonapartist pages. And then the rats, alas, had devoured three-quarters of the oration of Monseigneur the Archbishop of Angoulême; though we may feel sure that the weather was magnificent in that diocese dear to Heaven, and every heart agog with enthusiastic loyalty. "Vive, vive toujours notre cher Empereur Napoléon III!" But I should never discover anything more about "Movements of the Population"; it was the same with "Finances," whose shelf turned out to be entirely occupied by several folios of the Post-Office Directory. The "Drainage" section preserved, piously embalmed in a single small volume, the memories of several heroes of civil life; the "Horses" were coarser. Their file contained *La Garçonne* and *L'Album de Frou-frou*. "Taxes and Rebates" turned out to be seriously curtailed; revealing, beneath a layer of mouse-dirt, nothing but a copy of *Marion Delorme* and an ancient set

of Regulations of Louis-Philippe, badly dilapidated—
"Article 6. In future all materials of cotton, linen, or hemp
supplied for the various needs of His Majesty's Forces,
shall be marked throughout their length with stripes; the
numbers, colours, and dimensions of which shall be
determined by our Secretary of State for War..."

"Article 13. The position of the Senior Veterinary Sur-
geon in order of battle and order of march is two paces
to the left of the Medical Officers. The Assistant and
Deputy Assistant Veterinary Surgeons will march one
pace only to his rear..."

As to the "Correspondence for the Year," that file was
taken up simply and solely by the Prison Regulations of
1885—"Female prisoners shall be searched and examined
by persons of their own sex. Their vegetable soup shall
always be made with 15 grams of butter or 12 grams of
pork fat. The meat for their Sunday dinner shall *always*
consist of beef (or cow-meat, or mutton, or goat's flesh,
etc.). Their hair shall be cut every three months." That
at all events was precise.

Lastly, there protruded one final circular, this time in
typescript—"Very Urgent...inform us by post of the
number of subscriptions available for the *Golden Book of
Toll-Collectors*; for which the inclusive sum of three
francs, payable in one or more yearly instalments, can be
charged..."

And that was all! Function, thou "double functionary"!—however sorely tempted to cry "Eli, Eli,
Lama Sabachthani!"

⋆   ⋆   ⋆

When night fell, I at last found my predecessor, returned from a painful round of farewell visits, drooping
on a worm-eaten bench in the schoolroom, in the deepest
depression. He listened to my passionate complaints; he
struggled, it may be, to sympathize; but, poor devil, he
had troubles enough of his own. For a long while he sat
plunged in thought, though looking more as if he were
falling asleep; then, with a sudden wave of his arms,
"Well," he said in gloomy tones, "here's your future
domain—some antiquated tables, no proper school-
equipment... But never mind, you'll have no pupils
either; or if you do, by any chance, oh well, you'll
manage somehow! That old chest-of-drawers is your
bureau... Here, overhead, you have the names of the
three sons of the village who died for their country...
There now! In this place I have spent my whole career.
I wish you as much! That's all I can say."

"Very kind of you! But one thing I really should like
to know—what, once for all, *do* the duties of a Mayor's
Secretary consist in?"

"Oh, who knows?" he replied, gazing at the ceiling
and patting his crumpled coat. "Who knows?...You'll
have to trust to inspiration..."

"But still! You see—I really *must* ask you..."

Then, with sudden fury, he leapt up and strode about
the room, shouting: "They consist...they consist in
receiving every day a stack of incomprehensible docu-
ments; in replying anything you like to them; in having a
dust-up with the Tax-collector every time he calls; in
making returns of horse-drawn and motor vehicles in

2-2

which no one will ever take the slightest interest; in doing
every blessed job that Heaven sends; in being day and
night at everybody's beck and call; in distributing out-
door relief to women having babies, to the old, to paupers
and incurables who are in perfect health and better off
than you are yourself; in calling up, examining, black-
guarding, or getting illegal leave for conscripts and
reservists; in drawing up, auditing, and despatching in
quintuplicate communal budgets, electoral registers, returns of foreigners, figures of workers available; in keeping up to date the cadastral survey and the registers
belonging to it; in inventing statistics of every sort and
kind; in preventing, counteracting, or reporting crises of
unemployment, livestock epidemics, late frosts, hail-
storms, and conflagrations; in encouraging the silk-worm
industry by falsifying the weight of cocoons produced;
in looking after the fruit export-trade and the..."

"Mercy, mercy!"

"...in looking after the irrigation-system, the forests,
the crops, and the elections; in coping with victims of
disasters, poachers, smugglers, and marauders; in doing
all the work of the Assessors of Taxes, of the Drainage
Board, of the Relief Department, of the Police, of the
Council, of deputy and bottle-washer to the Mayor..."

"! ! !"

"...in forging everybody's signature; in stamping
everything in reach with the municipal stamp, without
ever struggling to understand..."

"! ! ! ! !"

"But, above all else—and mark my words—in never

hurrying yourself in the very least for the Government, the Commune, or the Electors; in hurling sys-tem-at-ic-al-ly into the fire all notices, circulars, summonses, letters, rigmaroles..."

"But..."

"...in doing your best, I tell you, to be damned well left in peace until you're pensioned off. That's the best a Mayor's Secretary on three hundred francs a year has to hope for; if he doesn't find elsewhere some slight private compensations of his own."

PLENARY SESSION

One evening in mid-October, as dusk was descending, I
received an official visit from the District Superintendent
of Roads.

In his celluloid choker, he had a look of the gravest
solemnity; and I realized at once that here was something
really important. As the only civil servant and the only
literary figure in the place, as the local correspondent of
the press, member for twenty years of the Municipal
Council, and actually more Mayor than the Mayor, he
had (he assured me) ideas of real grasp and insight on the
subject of our commune; he had, too, certain serious
projects for our welfare maturing in his brain; and he
had, into the bargain, a very vivid sense of his own
responsibilities.

Surely it could not somehow be this same sense of his
responsibilities that gave Théophile such a forbidding air.
No, that, as he pointed out to me, was due to my own lack
of *savoir vivre*. He was astonished, and with good reason
(he explained), that I had omitted on my arrival to call on
the important people in Mont-Paon. For a fortnight he
had waited in vain for that mark of my respect; then,
without bearing any malice, in the sacred cause of loyalty
between colleagues in the service, he had obligingly come
himself to enlighten me about the interests, prospects, and
personalities of our neighbourhood.

At this point in his exordium, wreathed in that cordial

smile of his, he made a pause; expecting of me some
apology, appreciation, exclamation of gratitude, or the
like—some sign that I had grasped what he was driving at.
But I had not grasped in the very least. Then, his smile
turning a little sour, he took a chair and with sharp gestures of his skinny hand, began expounding to me, willy-
nilly, the inner secrets of our municipality.

"This office of Mayor," he began, "is not what a
foolish Mayor imagines it to be." Then, to prove his
point, he set to work to interweave anecdotes and innuen-
does, suspicions and suppositions. I should find myself
dealing with a Mayor—an excellent fellow in himself, no
doubt—but uneducated...in a word, reactionary, quite
reactionary! As for the Municipal Council—oh, creatures of routine, mentalities absolutely medieval! Fortunately, there was himself, Théophile, on the spot—
always "pretty well on the spot"—to put his shoulder to
the wheel in the path of Progress and Civilization—"for
Civilization is on the march..."

"Yes, so someone called Pascal was saying."

At these words his moustache bristled. "Pascal? So
you have *already* seen Pascal?"

"At the Mayor's."

"At...ah!...and so they've been bringing you in
touch with the situation, have they!"

"Yes, with a good deal..."

"Indeed! Indeed!" He chewed furiously at his red
tooth-brush of a Charlie-Chaplin moustache. "So
they will have talked to you, no doubt, of...let me
see..."

"They talked about marriages, and drums, and notices, and elopements, and mock-serenades."

"Ah good, very good!" he exclaimed, his mind now set at rest. "Just topics of the moment, mere gossip. I was surprised that without me... Ah, my good madam, a Mayor's is an extremely serious position. I *know*—after standing in the breach here for more than thirty years! At this very moment, mark you, a vital question is brewing—that of Electric Lighting. I give you my word for it —we shall hear plenty about *that*!" There was a tone of menace in his voice, a look of philosophic gloom on his features. "What can you expect? Time moves us all on and, in spite of all our reactionaries, Mont-Paon is hungry for Progress. This place has had enough of candles and oil-lamps. It wants, at any price, electric lighting of its own—four lamps along the main road! Which we shall distribute as follows—one at each end of the village; the third in front of my door; the other one opposite the Big House. The new owner, you see, is a man to be considered. He has his ambitions; and at the coming elections he might want to turn us all out, and steal our shoes! Now, if my fourth lamp is put so as to light his drive, and supposing he *is* one day on the Council...enough said, I know what I'm about!" With satisfaction, this time, he rubbed his finger along his moustache; and then, swelling out his thin chest, he continued: "Under the pressure of the Progressive Party—represented by me—the Mayor has been forced to throw up the sponge and get drawn up—what shall I call it?"

"A plan and estimate from the Rural Board of Works. Oh I knew that too."

He gave a jump—"Ah, you knew? Well, one word
more! Whenever this plan arrives (and I shall see to it that
it does arrive, you can take my word for that), you will
at once summon the Council—the whole body—for a
Plenary Session; you will underline the fact that every
member's attendance is essential; then, you will wait for
me. It can't go ahead without me—this question of
electricity, which I was the first to start and have since kept
alive, concerns me directly! I'm on the look-out, taking
my steps and prepared for all emergencies. Now we shall
see if there is at last to 'be light' (one may well put it
so!) or whether our Reactionaries are to triumph '*in
vitam eternam*'!"

★   ★   ★

In theory, letters are delivered in Mont-Paon by the
Post Office of the chief town of the district; but in practice, by Théophile. His duties compel him to be constantly
travelling up and down Section 88 of the Route Nationale;
every day in the course of this function he meets the postman; and so, to save him the distance on his bicycle,
Théophile willingly takes over our village-mail. Then
with brotherly affection they stand each other a glass of
anisette, and everybody is happy.

Accordingly, for a fortnight on end, Théophile went
through the municipal correspondence with me, so as to
enlighten me, should I need it; and, as a matter of fact, to
see whether or no that plan from the Rural Board of
Works... It is too disgusting, the slackness of government
offices. And indeed the Board of Works was certainly
making fun of us. Unfailingly we kept receiving the
advertisements of the Abbé Soury, or of the Forty-four

Cures of the Abbé Magnat, or patterns of Sacred Hearts, suitable for wear, from a firm at Loretto; a whole battery of reactionary pietist organizations bombarded us with evangelical promises; the nuns of some Mont Sacré even offered to cure any of our children of bed-wetting... but the punctual arrival of an official document would have been miracle enough to cast all these in the shade. Mischievously the Mayor rubbed his hands and laughed at the Abbé Soury, at Théophile, at the paraffin-lamp that threw its light across our evening post—"Ah, la, la, who's ever going to see four electric lamps on the street of Mont-Paon!" But one evening—Oh calamity!—in its card-board case the famous Plan arrived! "Ah, what did I tell you? Now we shall see if Civilization..."

There, on lovely tracing-cloth, lay the cadastral plan of our commune, drawn in Indian ink and delicately colour-washed. Ah, what a charming commune it was! Green brooks tumbled in zigzags down the grey slopes of the Alpilles. The Roman Road—that triumphal thoroughfare now deep in dust, with its dislocated flagstones, over which high up the hill the twilight must be drawing now its fragile veil of mist—here shone out in fair black ink. What a dreamlike chess-board it all made, this plan; with our frog-tenanted marsh so delicately hatched, with its heraldic pine-woods and those tufted symbols for our olive-groves, with its cubic farm-houses on their earth-coloured ground and the twin towers of its château! There the railway crawled, like a sluggish caterpillar, amid the low vines; and the Route Nationale, patterned with plane-trees, wriggled on its way trying to shake off their

weight. But a stealthy arrow had pierced our Grand-
Paon, with its peacock-tuft of black pines; a red circle had
wounded its iridescent neck of olive-groves; and thence a
scarlet thread descended to the road, along whose sym-
bolic whiteness it burst into four flaming stars. These,
according to the legend beneath, were our long dreamt-
of transformer, its copper wire, and finally the four lamps
that would keep watch over our quiet slumbers. This was
what Pascal called "Progress on the march"; and what
our Superintendent, the journalist of Mont-Paon, had
described as "the puissant electric Fairy, bringing light
and joy into the humblest cot."

Accordingly I sent out the summonses for a Plenary
Session—inviting, urging, insisting, underlining; then
I waited for Saturday evening.

On Saturday evening in the Council Room I waited
for the Councillors.

It was one of those days when nothing will go right;
when, as the saying goes, the Devil blows into the saucepan. Assuredly he was blowing into that Council Room
with a quite infernal uproar. The whole place shook,
creaked, and swayed on its foundations; only there was
nothing to be seen, for the hanging paraffin-lamp refused
to function. Its Prussian nozzle would not tolerate at all
the glass-chimney, inscribed with the trade-mark "Sun of
France", which had been set over it. Viciously it regur-
gitated its own flame, spitting smuts of all sizes on to the
ten municipal chairs that stood there, stiff with boredom.
So I waited for the Councillors. But the Councillors did
not come.

Finally there was a sound of wooden shoes groping and
stumbling on the stairs; then, black in the yet blacker
frame of the doorway, appeared a round-shouldered
silhouette, recognizable by its large hooded cape and its
cap with ear-flaps. The Mayor—for it was he—made a
tour of the room in the smoke-laden obscurity, bumped
into the armchair where reposed the drum, invoked the
name of the Lord, gazed out through the dim windows at
the dimmer night and the great groaning cypresses,
listened to the weathercock screaming overhead like a
wounded peacock, then came back to the lamp in a state
of general disgust. "Filthy weather for our autumn
beans!—what in the name of God do we want with this
lighting-system! Are you really set on holding the
Council in here?"

"Set on it...no! But isn't this the Council Room?"

"It's whatever one chooses it to be! Your predecessor
used it to sleep in! Take my word for it, we shall be more
comfortable in the Schoolroom, in the ordinary way.
There must be a few candle-ends left over from the last
wedding. They'll do better anyway than this filthy 'Im-
proved Lamp'."

In the Schoolroom, the same darkness, the same din.
On the rickety chest-of-drawers that served as desk, two
candle-ends stuck on either margin of that exquisite
cadastral plan guttered lamentably. They would never
last out our Plenary Session! And in fact, at the very
moment when the Progressive Party opened the door—
Pascal hard on the heels of the Superintendent—the
shorter candle-end of the two flared up in the draught and

blew out with a nauseating stench. Its companion continued to make terrific efforts to meet our needs. At the
entry of Jean de Jacques it even surpassed itself—sent a
yellow radiance dancing all over the new-comer's gro-
tesquely battered hat, his knife-edged nose, his ferret's
face—then all at once, like a heroic candle-end that has
performed the impossible, collapsed into a sticky blob of
grease. And now hob-nailed boots went stumbling into
tables, there was a series of curt but vigorous exclamations,
somebody coughed, the chest-of-drawers groaned under
the impact of a wooden shoe. "Come along," I said,
"into the kitchen! We shall at least be warm there, and
able to see..."

"Rather irregular," laughed Théophile, "still one must
bow to circumstances. Ah, once we get our electric
light!"

The kitchen, with its trusty lamp and its great fire of
almond-wood, seemed to them all a harbour of refuge.
Here the raging of the storm outside sank to a soft rumble
in the chimney. Hands were stretched out towards the
flames; tense faces relaxed in the firelight. Gaily chair
bumped against chair, more gaily still chinked the cups of
coffee and the little glasses of brandy served out by a joking
Pascal. We had escaped at last from cold and darkness.
But the Devil has more than one trick up his sleeve; and
we could not escape that cadastral plan or its accompanying specifications—its copper wire, posts, masonry,
and insulators of porcelain. No choice—opened they had
to be, there in the centre of the table. At once our cor-
diality faltered and grew cold. What bitter altercations

were not these innocent-looking papers about to pro-
voke! Jean de Jacques, already deep in a discussion about
sowing, stopped open-mouthed, his hand in his seed-
basket; the Superintendent of Roads, all smiles till now,
knitted his forehead; the Mayor, pretending to notice
nothing, held up against the light his little glass of eau-de-
vie. Even Pascal, taken aback by this sudden silence,
allowed some far-fetched pleasantry to die upon his lips,
then lapsed into sentiment—"After all, we're all related here, we've all known each other since we were
born..."

A bad sign, that sentimentality. And a heavy strain, this
silence. But by good luck at that moment appeared Zène.
For a single instant he stopped short on the threshold.
Motionless there in his brown corduroys, smiling under
his broad-brimmed felt-hat with a basket of apples beneath his arm, he looked like an image of some kindly
country saint entering Bethlehem, on a pedestal of clay.
He bumped into Jean de Jacques, and smiled; he caught
his basket in Pascal's chair, and smiled; then, depositing
his offering in one corner, "They're just some pippins for
you," said he. "Oh, terribly poor pippins! They're all
dropping with the maggot. But baked with honey—well,
perhaps, though I won't say for sure...Or if you made
some apple-tea..."

At these blessed words, by this happy irruption of
noise, gesture, and speech, the fatal spell of silence was
broken, the Evil One exorcised. At once the hands of
Jean de Jacques returned to his seed-basket; Pascal with
vivid gestures of make-believe began busily digging in

dumb-show among his manure; and then how he made
it rain and rain! So that Sylvestre, opening the door,
received full in his face a scattered handful of phantom
corn and the imaginary drops of that downpour of
Pascal's dream. He stumbled out of the way towards
Zène in the window-recess; and there, in low tones and
half-gestures, shy but happy, they both settled down to
discuss the treatment of swellings in rabbits.

"Well," said the Mayor all of a sudden, "suppose we
begin, as we're all here?"

"All?"—I pointed to the places still empty.

"Oh, as for those four..."—everybody laughed.

"There's the Long Stammerer"—said Pascal.

"Who dreads electricity like the plague," broke in the
Superintendent of Roads. "He's been told—God knows
who by—that the current attracts lightning and gives you
pneumonia. Catch *him* coming!"

The Mayor smiled, embarrassed by this veiled allusion
to himself. "Then there's Pierre from the Mas du Diable
—but his mare's very bad, he wouldn't be leaving her
alone for a trifle like this."

"Then there's my brother-in-law," continued Théophile. "But as we don't see eye to eye, and I *always*
attend meetings, no fear of his ever coming."

As for the last absentee of the four...but no one could
think who this last could be. "Why, it's Liffran," cried
Zène, beaming. There was a general burst of laughter—

"Why yes, of course, Liffran..."

"Liffran?"

"What, you don't know Liffran yet?"

"An old shepherd..."

"Who lives up the mountain..."

"The husband of Bernade..."

"An old man, bent double, past eighty..."

"Drags his wooden shoes, as he walks, and wears a great woollen coat..."

"He goes by every day with his flock..."

"And every evening with his wheelbarrow..."

"We put him on to make a tenth—but, poor old thing, you can guess *he* never comes," added the Superintendent of Roads.

"He just agrees to everything!"

"And doesn't care a damn about anything!"

"He's so out of the world, right out of it."

The Meeting began.

As one man, they bent their heads over the blue and brown plan of their commune, astonished and thrilled to see it all there—so tiny, so neat, so beautifully squared.

"But," asked Sylvestre dubiously, "where is my house?"

"There!" said the Superintendent of Roads, laying his autocratic finger on the ruined chapel. "And here's your road!" As this supposed road was really the irrigation-canal, it took Sylvestre quite a long time to identify his own property. However, he succeeded in the end. Then, one after the other, they all set about looking for their own vines, their own barns...and at this point things failed to satisfy them. What! This barbed-wire entanglement of crosses—could it be really the pine-wood? These mis-shapen cubes, their houses? These tiny squares, their broad acres? Their lands were all marked too small, their boundaries inexact, their stables in the wrong places.

"Well, here's the Mairie, anyway!" resumed Jean de Jacques, pressing his nail on the barn of the Big House. "And here's the way the electricity goes."

"No, no! Look, follow the wire!" explained the Mayor. "See, here it goes—across...a meadow...?"

"Not at all! Along by the marsh!"

Théophile was growing irritated. "It's perfectly simple," said he. "The wire just follows the Roman Road. I've got it, look! Then it turns—"

"You've not got it at all. You're muddling up the road with the railway. Here it is, your wire! No mistaking it —see, it's marked red. It passes close by the *mas* of—"

"Not a bit of it!" cried the Mayor, obstinately following a quite different track. "You've got right into the middle of the oak-wood where the truffles grow!"

I had to fold up the plan altogether and, while they marched in imagination over the solid ground, to picture the whole thing to them from memory—first of all, in the neck of the Grand-Paon stood that barbed arrow, our long dreamt-of transformer, painted with its skulls and cross-bones; then, bit by bit, I unrolled that long glistening wire which had tripped up Sylvestre. "It takes the line of the Roman Road. You follow? Then along the cypresses..."

"Ah yes, the cypresses of Edouard! Very good—go ahead."

"Now we come down to a brook there..."

"The Big Brook! Exactly!"

"At the cross-roads it turns north... You still follow?"

"Yes, that's all right."

"No, I'm lost," admitted Zène with a smile.

"But look here—"

"Oh no," said he quietly, "your wire won't pass any-where near me, that was all I wanted to know. So far as everything else is concerned, do whatever you like." And he began carefully rubbing off a speck of dried mud that blemished the finest apple in his basket.

"You mean, you give your approval, you're on the side of Progress, eh?" asked Théophile.

"Mon dieu, yes, provided it doesn't go too far."

"Nothing goes too far, when one has real determination. Capacity for self-sacrifice... that's what Progress means!"

"Hear, hear!" echoed Pascal. "We must go ahead. The whole village is in favour. Our children must be able to say—"

The Mayor burst into a roar of laughter. "Steady, old man! Don't forget you're a bachelor! Never mind about your children—we must get on with *this*, if we don't want to be here all night!"

Once more the wire pursued its course, turning corners, leaping gaps, or getting tangled up; until finally our four lamps starred the road with their golden aureoles, Théophile rubbed his hands, and everybody drew a deep breath of satisfaction. Reaction was defeated. "Very well," sighed the Mayor, resigned, "let's pass a vote in favour and have done with it, then go to bed."

But alas our Meeting was not over yet. It remained to read and approve the estimate of the Chief Engineer. At

this point Sylvestre with his wooden shoes got hopelessly
stuck in the difference between four-millimetre and six-
millimetre wire. The mouth of Jean de Jacques grew tight,
articulating alternate acceptance and rejection of no one
quite knew what—"high voltage," "maximum tensions,"
"circuit-breakers"... Porcelain and telegraph-poles, it
appeared, had trebled their prices in the last three years—
that was all that the Mayor took in. At every pause I could
see Zène smiling at his unseen angels and the Superintendent of Roads gnawing his moustache... "From which
it follows," concluded the estimate, "that the installation
of the four lamps as specified will cost the said commune
the lump sum of a hundred and twenty-seven thousand
francs, eighty-three centimes, apart from extras..."
That at least they all understood; and, all except Zène,
with a violent start.

"Good Lord!" whistled Pascal, despite himself.

"What!" laughed the Mayor. "'Capacity for self-
sacrifice, *that's* what Progress means'—as we've just been
hearing!"

Sylvestre, who had grasped nothing except this total,
spat heavily on the floor—"You could buy a good few
candles for that!" said he.

"As for me," burst out Jean de Jacques, "I'm like the
man of Auriol,* I don't care a damn. I live too far out for

* Auriol is a village near Aubagne (Bouches-du-Rhône).
Everyone at Aubagne was praying hard for rain—all except one
man. "Why aren't you on your knees?" said the priest. "We
shan't get rain, if we don't pray for it." "Oh," replied the man,
"I'm from Auriol, much I care about your rain!" Whence the
phrase has become proverbial.

your four lamps to be much good to me. And then I always go to bed with the sun. But if you want my opinion, it's this. I'll never sign a paper for a hundred and twenty-seven thousand francs, just to light up the drive of the Big House. I'm a plain-spoken man, I am. And I find it just a little too expensive, to oblige a few citizens at this sort of rate. Théophile, mon vieux, if you want to see your way about at night, you just buy a lantern; and you, Pascal, if you find the road dark on your way home from the café, just you go to bed a little sooner and razzle-dazzle a little less. You'll be all the better for it!"

"Don't be so pig-headed, and confuse the discussion," replied Pascal with a laugh. "My razzle-dazzling is one thing, electricity's quite another. We've got to vote 'Yes' or 'No,' and to think well beforehand. We shall never get anything done, if money stops us. After all, what are a hundred and twenty thousand francs in these days? Just a mosquito in a lion's mouth!"

"Fffffu! The rate you go at! You've got to have the money first, before you can spend it! As well try squeezing the stones of la Crau!—you'll get neither blood nor gold out of them!"

"We'll put it on the rates."

"Sch-ch-ch!"

"We'll borrow it."

"A pretty notion, upon my word!" cried Sylvestre.

"We'll ask for a State-subsidy!"

"You first find the cash for us, you clever fellows; and then we'll discuss it again."

"But we've *been* discussing it for years. We shall always be back-numbers—stick-in-the-muds..."

"Bumpkins..."

"But," persisted Jean de Jacques, "beggars we are and beggars we always shall be, Pascal; and that's the whole truth of it."

Under cover of this debate Sylvestre and Zène had taken up again from the start the question of the treatment of swellings in rabbits; and now they were softly making for the door. Théophile, full of scorn, shrugged his shoulders and let them go their way. Pascal kept up his running denunciation of the spirit of routine, simultaneously gripping the Mayor by his coat and Jean de Jacques by one arm. "You understand... we *must* march with the times." But Jean de Jacques was now marching towards the door; while the Mayor shrugged his shoulders, repeating: "A hundred and twenty-seven thousand francs, do you hear, a hundred and twenty-seven thousand francs, and not one sou in our chest!"

"Civilization..." reiterated Théophile.

But by now, the Reactionaries were feeling more ribald than ever about "Civilization." Finally, determined to have done with it, Jean de Jacques wrenched himself free from the grasp of Pascal, turned his back, pulled up the collar of his tight coat and, tugging his battered hat down over his eyes, "No, no, I tell you, no!" he shouted. "Let me go in peace."

"But haven't you grasped the importance...?"

No; but he had firmly grasped the latch. Then the Party of Progress, leaving the Mayor to his obscurantism, clung fast, one on the right, the other on the left, to the shoulders of Jean de Jacques, and with him crossed the threshold. The open door, caught by the wind, slammed with all its force behind the trio. Then, suddenly, silence.

Left alone in front of the now spotted and blotted cadastral plan, the Mayor shook his head, and rubbed his chin with a thoughtful air. His arms behind his back, he stumped round the lighted room, made for the window, and contemplated through its glass, with great amusement, those three shadow-shapes still waving, arguing, battling with the storm, under the wavering pallor of the newly risen moon. For a moment he seemed listening for the shadows' voices; but the weathercock overhead, with its wounded peacock's scream, and the groaning of the great cypresses drowned all other sounds. Then he marched back to the lamp, delighted. "Had a success, eh, with our Plenary Session? The only bore is that we shall still have to pay for that Engineer and all his stationery! But never mind! I shall be only too glad, even though it costs us a hundred francs; yes, a hundred francs on the special expenses of the commune—you may take my word that, for a lesson like this, I'd think the money well spent!"

THE QUINQUENNIAL CENSUS

"I have the honour," said the buff circular, "to forward you under this cover the necessary forms for the Quinquennial Census of the population and buildings of your commune; together with the dockets, returns, counterfoil-books, nominal-rolls and receipt-forms relating thereto, which you will have the kindness to fill up in accordance with the law of March 25th, 1885, and the decrees of Jan. 11th and 20th, 1904.

"I attach the greatest weight to the accuracy of this investigation, the national importance of which will be self-evident to you; and also to the promptitude of your returns. You will forward me lists and register with the shortest possible delay. The census-officials who show most assiduity in collecting census-returns are eligible for honorary distinctions, decorations, or diplomas. Kindly acknowledge receipt of this by post to the 15th Division, 3rd Bureau, 1st Section of the Department..."

On principle, and in accordance with a custom rapidly acquired, I crumpled into a tight ball this piece of Prefectural prose and flung it to blacken on the hearth, where so many others had blackened before it. I refrained from sending any acknowledgement, I merely waited for events to take their course and for the arrival of that fateful seventh of March—the day appointed for my display of promptitude, the day when my returns would gladden the hearts of the lovers of statistics, perhaps gain me a

diploma, and preserve at the required degree of exaltation
the morale of my country.

In my heart, indeed, I prayed that the fall of the
Ministry, a geological cataclysm, a Fascist coup d'état, or
my own suspension might deliver me from the horrors
of that fatal day. But once governments get it into their
heads to take a census, nothing will ever really get it
out again; and even if Philippe V had reconquered
his throne, whatever else he levelled with the dust,
though still swimming in the blood of revolution, he
would none the less have exacted this census of our
population.

And so on Sunday, the seventh of March, the sun rose
at the appointed hour; and operations commenced.
Hardly a soul in our administrative district had read
through, taken in, or filled up that meticulous questionnaire. Each of them arrived, at his own good time,
bringing his blue form, quite blank of any information,
but liberally stained with oil or petrol, mud or finger-
marks. The Mayor, in his efforts to clear up the case of each
householder, was busy confusing buildings with cadastral
numbers, losing himself in the distinctions between
ordinary tenants and tenants paying in kind, sighing,
swearing, and quite unable to answer the questions cease-
lessly reiterated by the aggrieved victims. For, good
souls, none of them can understand "why, every now and
then, do they so pester poor mankind?"

"Is it because we don't pay taxes enough, that they
can't let us alone? They can just fill up our forms themselves if they want them," growled Jean de Jacques,

spitting indignantly. And he flung me his sky-blue forms to fill up instead of Them.

Next came the Long Stammerer, suspicious and exasperated. "The qu-questions they a-ask one, you know . . . !"—the vehemence of his gesture conveyed that his patience was at an end. "Why the n-name of my wi-wife? The year of my m-marriage? My barn, my st-stable! What the d-devil do they wa-want to do with them, I should like to know!" When he was further told that they wanted to know also how many rooms he occupied and whether his mother-in-law lived with him, he exploded: "That'll do, that'll do! That's no-nobody's business! If anyone w-wants to know more, let him c-come and see me—and I'll give him a welcome!"

"But it's for reasons of hygiene!"

"What! Hy-Hygiene! What sort of hocus-pocus is that? Come now, I've eyes in my h-head—I know that the end of it will just be that they raise our t-taxes."

"How many children?"

"You know. Two, and a third on the w-way!"

"Any other dependants? Any aged relatives living with you? Any —"

"Oh, d-damn it, no! I shift for myself, eh! My relatives will jolly well d-do the same!" Ramming his hat down on his head, his extinguished cigarette-end clinging to his lip, off he went, stammering his oaths and cursing for stuffed owls the Government and me, alas, its representative.

Then appeared a dark cloak, edging cautiously towards my table From inside its hood, drawn tight though

spring was now so near, emerged first of all a convulsion
of coughing; and then, little by little, the bushy countenance of Liffran. The old shepherd's tousled hair, his
tangled beard and moustache, suggest alike the curly hair
of a sheep-dog and the fleece of a ram. By long association
with his beasts he has acquired that placidity and impassivity which leave the impression of profound wisdom.

"It's still this catarrh of mine up to its old tricks,"
groaned Liffran; and proceeded to describe to us in minute
detail how he "felt the mother mounting in him,"* how
it made him short-winded when he walked, choked him
when he slept, and when he got out of breath, completely
strangled and suffocated him. "I've tried everything, I've
swallowed raw snails, I've kept on my chest the skin of a
snake killed in June, I've put shave-grass in my shoes—
nothing's any good. With me the worms've got into the
wood, that's all. And then as for these papers, said I to
myself, as for these census-papers...??? So I've just
brought them to you—you'll know more about such
things. Till next time, then; good morning, everybody!"
Alas, poor Liffran, your catarrh will not be good enough
for the census-officials. Our unconscionable questions,
penetrating with difficulty his rough cloak and tangled
hair, left him dismayed and disconsolate. "Ah, my
friends, it isn't that I'm not willing, but how on earth can
I tell exactly...I must be seventy-six—seventy-eight—
eighty, maybe...? It's such a long time! Oh, as for

* "La mère" *i.e.* choking. Cf. Shakespeare, *Lear* II. 4. 56:
    O! how this mother swells up toward my heart;
    Hysterica passio! Down, thou climbing sorrow!

Bernade, that's quite simple. She's just three or four
years younger than me. Her birthday's on St Joseph's
Day."

Our rough calculations seemed to cause him a tranquil
pleasure. "The date of my marriage? Oh, you're just
laughing at me! Wait a moment, now...I did a year in
the army—only one, being a widow's son; then I came
back home—to Briançon—up in the Alps. And I stayed
there—oh, mon dieu, two years, three years, maybe...?
Then my cousin, who'd set up near Avignon—folk were
doing well here then, at market-gardening—sent for me
to come down and join him. So I came—after my
mother'd died; but I still went on being a shepherd. And
then—after a year or so, come harvest time, I got married. There!...that must make it about...oh, I can't tell,
just you work it out as you think."

"And how old are your children?"

"Oh that!—that's easy. Jeanne, she's the eldest. She
was born almost at once...eh, yes, mon dieu, that same
year...four or five months after we got married...
things will happen so. Then we lost two. So, according to
that Maria would be three—no, four—no, three years
younger than her, bless me. That's it. She was born the
fifteenth of August. Then the twins; then Jean, who's
doing his military service now—he was confirmed along
with Pierre from the Mas Neuf. Ah yes, my good lady,
we've had our share—of children; and my youngest girl's
going on just the same way. She doesn't know what it is,
but...what do you expect?...it's just nature."

The questions done, he pulled his hood of serge down

over his eyes again, smiled with his large toothless mouth, coughed, and rubbing his ribs trudged painfully away.

"Ma qué?" cried from the doorway, at the same moment, the Italian from the Château. "Vat business you vant with my childrens? My vife, she have had nine; and she have nursed—besides—dieci! Volete—or no?— sapere also ze children zat vimmen have *nursed*? Ma qué, zat is nothing to laugh; zat is great bother! The eldest son, he is Terzilio. Say...quaranta sette. Me?—sixty next month. Nunziata, she—"

"What, you mean to say you're sixty, and yet...!"

"Yes, madonna! Sixty, or sixty-two—"

"And you mean to tell me you're only thirteen years older than your own son!"

"Christo! Ma who tell you that Terzilio be mine? He is my vife's, by a first marriage. And I, by another mar- riage—I have tre altri; and, by her, we have again quatro. Ma senti, signora? Nunziata—she is so much older than me—twenty year, perhaps. She is old woman. Ma, Dio, what folly of me, when I was young and a widow!"

"Then who lives in the Château?"

"Ma all of us! There is vork for her children, and for mine, and for ze sons-in-law and ze daughters-in-law, and for ze little ones also, quando they shall be big."

"How many rooms?"

"Vat, you really vant to know that too, eh? For why so much of questions? Because I am foreign? Put down four or five—sta bene!"

"What, four or five rooms in a Château with three

floors, lived in by ten families! You're just making fun of us!"

"Ma, sacré Dio, ze second floor and ze third, and even ze first, zey are never opened! Senti? It is so many lavatories and billiard-rooms. You think ve vant all these billiards, all these bathrooms? Put five rooms, I tell you! —e poi, listen, if you want twenty francs—you too, like ze minister, then say so and it is done! Twenty francs from every house-holder, from every French, from every Italian, it you will! Ma not so many questions! Not so many papieri! Not so many forms! All ze money of France, it just go on papieri, blue or verdi!"

At this point, the Italian's tenant-farmer, weary of waiting for his tirade to finish, handed me his own roll of papers over the shoulders of the Lord of the Manor— "Here are my returns. They're all filled up. I'm used to it all."

The old Italian turned on him, furious. "Hey, you are used to it? You are lucky man, to be used to censuses! But, hey, why you no tell me?—You could have filled up mine also and spare me that great trouble!"

Right into the evening we had to go battling on— filling up returns, or cooking them; giving assurances to one that the census was not a mobilization, to another that it had nothing to do with new schemes of taxation; explaining to the sceptical and the suspicious that it was merely intended that we should waste a fine Sunday— that, the object of the Government being to give the greatest possible trouble to the largest possible number of people, for once they had succeeded perfectly. Then a

worthy mother of a family had to be persuaded to delete
the name of her eldest son—away on foreign service at
Bizerta—from the list of those at home, with a solemn
promise that the ominous line of black ink would not
bring the young man to disaster. A blind eye had to be
turned to the strange circumstance that a "war-orphan"
did not know who was her own father; and that the
Spanish couple recently taken on at the Big House were
living together as man and wife.

After dinner, a few late-comers still kept arriving. "On
the way to the café it's no trouble to drop in here," remarked a wood-cutter. "But if there's any more information you want, come to the *mas* to-morrow, it'll be
a nice little walk for you. And if I'm out, you'll find me all
right in one valley or another. I'm cutting pines all over
the mountain now."

That night of March 7th was haunted by nightmares,
blue or pink, in packets of five hundred, requiring to be
filled up with the most devastating information.

Next day at dawn there was a violent battering on the
door. Had they come to check the falsity of my returns,
or to award me a diploma? No, it was only a few last
papers being handed in—"as we're on our way down to
sow potatoes, it's no trouble to return you your forms—
if forms are what make you happy!"

And when a little later, my courage gone, I was
floundering among piles of statistics, dreaming of dis-
missal and degradation and full of remorse for having,
once upon a time, despised and derided poor officials, the
Superintendent of Roads handed me an enormous pack-

age, entrusted to him by the railway-station in the
neighbouring town. It was accompanied by a letter,
bearing the stamp of the Prefecture, as follows: "I have
the honour to forward you under the same cover the
white and yellow forms on which should be made the
returns of information demanded by the decree of Decem-
ber 8th from all foreign proprietors in your commune.
The national importance of this information will be self-
evident to you; and you will be so good as to handle them
with that promptitude and accuracy which they require.
These returns should be rendered in quintuplicate. In
drawing them up, you will follow the cadastral originals;
then, in collaboration with the Immigration Commission,
the Inspector of Taxes, the Collector of Taxes, and your
Municipal Council, whose decisions, with their full
reasons, you will report in triplicate, you will draw up
your summary and report, and render the same, with the
briefest possible delay, to the 8th Bureau, 4th Division...
Kindly acknowledge receipt by post..."

Lacking even energy enough to crumple into a ball this
sea-green circular, I seized a stray pen still wet from my
desk and, with spirit broken, wrote: "I have the honour
to acknowledge receipt of..."

WORMS AND PALMS

Over Section 88 of the Route Nationale that winds its way between Mont-Paon and the neighbouring town, there reigns the most distinguished figure in our whole commune—Théophile, our Superintendent of Roads.

Whether he is wearing a cap of the latest spring-fashion, or an ample Balaclava helmet, or the jauntiest of straw-hats; whether he is dressed in overcoat, cloak, or jacket—even if he should have lost his celluloid collar or assumed a disguise—Théophile remains always Théophile, with a manner that is all his own.

What sort of power, indeed, could the clumsy and superficial capriciousness of mere costume ever possess to disguise the owner of those twisted legs ("Louis-Quinze legs," as an erudite painter once called them); of that jerky gait, like some elderly sergeant's; of that sinister protruding jaw, that mouth, those gimlet eyes beneath their receding brows; of that cunning, insolent complacency which in every feature and every gesture cries out—"I am Somebody. I am an Official. The world is powerless against *me!*"

In himself Théophile is changeless—marble—bronze. He is eternal. The only changes are in the attributes his right hand wields—puissant and familiar symbols, varying with place and season. At one moment brandishing an iron notice in his fist, he indicates to users of the road that it is, for weeks to come, "Under Repair." To all protests he replies, eloquently dumb, with a mere lift of his eye-brows. You will only be jolted to pieces on his road-metal, or burst your tyres; what do you suppose he cares? If he drops his notice, to take out a propelling-pencil, then, road-menders, beware! He is going to calculate the cubic volume of road-metal laid down, and thereby catch you out. But if, cocking his fountain-pen behind his ear, he snatches the shovel from your hands, just to show you "the right way to scatter sand," then resign yourselves; you will be reported to the Board and no one can say if you will ever see promotion again. On the rare days when a steam-roller is at work on the road, Théophile becomes a dictator, a generalissimo. He grasps, waves, brandishes the red flag of the Department of Roads and Bridges, blocks the road at his own high pleasure, and with a gesture from which there is no appeal, holds up the most mettlesome of carriage-horses, or cars all snorting with arrogance. "I don't care if you're the Minister in person—there's nothing for it but to take the by-road." And his steam-roller has simply to stand its ground. Then he lifts a forefinger—no more; and the obedient monster advances, retires, advances again.

Unfortunately on Section 88 there blows a wind of anarchism and insubordination, so that often on its plane-trees, or on some notice of "Work in Progress," the Superintendent finds freshly scrawled in charcoal some virulent invective, or evil-sounding stanza at his own expense. Then, with a mixture of bitterness and pride, he turns to contemplate his insulted flag, his propelling-pencil, his pocket note-book. "The moment," he

observes, "that one exerts a *scrap* of authority" (but, as he
utters it, how that "scrap" seems to expand upon his very
tongue!), "one becomes the target for ingratitude and
calumny!"

But on certain other mornings, the attributes of his
dignity laid aside, he may be seen traversing Mont-Paon
with a set of post-cards held fan-wise in his fingers. It is
merely that the idle postman at the neighbouring town
has trusted him with our letters. "After all, it's such a
little matter...and when one *can* be useful..." Whether
or no there lies behind this pretty gesture some deeper and
more private motive, you will find out for yourselves
some day (and soon at that), O benevolent and un-
suspicious souls who are moved to exclaim anew—
"What a good fellow he is, this Théophile—so kind to
poor country-postmen!" Very human he becomes, on
days like this, our Superintendent of Roads. He—the one
official functionary of the neighbourhood—condescends
for our benefit to abdicate his high estate and deliver our
letters and newspapers, accepting in return—(for it is such
a mistake to be stiff)—accepting cordially and without
ceremony a glass of *pastis* or just a drop of rum—" *Ah non,
merci*, I never drink anything sweet!"

It may even happen that Théophile will be seen striding
along with empty hands. At such times he wears a more
preoccupied look—a certain air of mystery, resolution,
importance. He is on his way to cure a case of worms!

★   ★   ★

Whenever, within a radius of several leagues, a child grinds his teeth in his sleep, if he has a bleared look about the eyes and his eye-lashes turned up, then they send for Théophile—"the Worm-Doctor." The really credulous souls of the Provençal La Vendée, wealthy and deferential, even come themselves to fetch him in a taxi or a market-cart. Among them he feels in his element. It is with an air of the deepest concentration that he performs his exorcisms, directing the worms by the shortest route home to their proper "pocket"—a pocket, as everybody knows, situated underneath the ribs. He invokes the God of Grubs, crosses himself three times, patters off his formulas. Rejoice, good people!—it has been uphill work this time; but he can guarantee a cure. Next, he has a rabbit flayed alive and, gabbling his Paternosters faster than ever, applies the still warm skin to the infant's chest. "Now," says he with a supercilious air, "you can keep some leek-poultices applied to the orifice of the stomach. But he's turned the corner all right by now. We were just in time!... As for payment, that I leave to you. I'm not grasping...still, of course, one must live!" The super-stitious are always open-handed. But he finds things very different among the "enlightened" population of the Valley—"that nest of free-thinkers and communists." Devoid as they are of the very rudiments of good man-ners, they just summon Théophile by post, naming day and hour; and even then they indulge in endless pleasan-tries at his expense. It may even be that they send for him merely to make fun of him! None the less Théophile pays his visit; but he pays it without pomp or circumstance.

He arrives on an old bicycle, officiates without rabbit-skins, poultices, or Low Masses, hazards the learned term "congexion" (which is safely non-committal), applies a vigorous massage to the patient's stomach, prescribes a dose of grog or aspirin, and... "that will be fifteen francs, if you please, for medical attention."

But under all the heady champagne of his glory there lies, inevitably, one bitter drop of ipecacuanha—in Mont-Paon itself no one ever asks him to treat their worms. Not indeed—Heaven be praised!—that in Mont-Paon worms are unknown or despised. On the contrary! Nowhere in the great world are worms more dreaded. But, instead of believing in boiled leek-poultices, Mont-Paon holds by raw garlic; it asks nothing better; and, mon dieu, it will have nothing else. For this charming village is, alas, heretical. Where others wear the blue ribbon of the Blessed Mary, its children go about in necklaces of garlic-cloves: then, during the moon's wane, they all lunch off a hunk of break rubbed with garlic and moistened with olive-oil; and the worms find that sufficient notice. "Here you have," growls the exasperated Théophile, "here you have a crying example of the havoc of a hide-bound tradition! Bread rubbed with garlic indeed! Strengthening for the stomach?—oh, no doubt! Good for a salad?—oh, as much as you like! But to make a *remedy* of it! They might as well use Chiarini's vermifuge! Which is about as much good as a plaster on a wooden leg! But it's not for want of lectures from me about it—fossils that they are!" No, indeed, it is not for want of lectures from Théophile. While he is delivering the day's letters (one must be

obliging), there occur such golden opportunities for
poking stomachs, peering at tongues, preaching to the
poor in spirit! Such brilliant diagnoses ensue, such sound-
ings of chests, such proposals for poultices! But no,
Mont-Paon has too firm a faith in garlic. It refuses all his
baits. For Théophile, in his efforts to be seductive, has
also concocted certain other little specialities (God forgive
him!)—has profaned the purity of Science with various
doubtful practices that border on heresy, Black Magic,
and sheer charlatanism. He is able, he claims, to expel an
Arles fever with a pinch of red powder steeped in rain-
water; to charm away sunstroke with a glass balanced on
your head; or to rid your bronchial tubes of any treacherous chill. He can disentangle in a second the nerves that
have got twisted over your stomach; he can make
women's milk come; he can, if you wish...but no,
Mont-Paon does not wish. Mont-Paon, indeed, does not
feel any doubt or derision towards his red ochre (one
remedy is doubtless as good as another); but, just as it
persists in stringing together its garlic necklaces, so it goes
on gathering on the Alpilles its "Alpine tea," against
chills and fevers; its herbs for toothache; its flowers for
sore eyes; its spike-lavender and agrimony to cure whit-
lows; and then, to avoid sun-strokes, all the summer
through, during "the middle hours" it just takes a siesta
in the shade. Thus, in its innocent and artless good nature,
does his native village poison the whole existence of its
Superintendent of Roads.

For what does it signify to be the most distinguished
figure in the place, the only man in it of education and

ability, the one official in a collar of celluloid—what does
it signify to be its Mayor's right hand, its Party of Progress, the foremost on its Council, the mainspring of its
administration, the sole representative of the Department
of Roads and Bridges, the local correspondent of all the
Radical press—what does it signify to be feared, courted,
consulted, respected, and admired, if in spite of everything such old wives' remedies continue to defy you!
And there is more behind (and here lies the political
secret, the ulcer at the heart of Théophile, the insurgent
Worm that no exorcism can lure back into its "pocket")
—what profits anything—all this reputation, all these
empty glories—if he is never to wear the oxidized chain
that lies loose in our Municipal drawer? Neither to heal,
nor to hold office! Not to be able to dominate a village
of a hundred and twenty souls! Honours fall lightly
enough to the incapable; but to him, "the man of
emergencies," only the most thankless tasks. For, in
short, who is it that makes the Municipal Council meet,
proceed, vote? Who carries on a campaign of intrigue in
the cause of electricity? Who is the adviser, guide, and
pilot of the Mayor, when the pair of them go to Marseilles to elect a Senator? Who, in a few well-chosen
words, replies to the Prefect? And finally, when some
great personage strays into Section 88, who welcomes
him at the Municipal Building, after hoisting with his own
hands our large moth-eaten flag? Théophile, always
Théophile. But in vain. Each election is a fresh blow to
him. His wounded pride, indeed, has invented a plau-
sible excuse—"No salaried state-servant," he says, "can

be officially Mayor. The law forbids." "Hardly!"—
comes the answer, "supposing Mont-Paon really wanted
you." But, in fact, just as it prefers garlic to leek-
poultices and sage-tea to red ochre, this perverse, guileless
village prefers to all the push of Théophile its good-
natured Mayor—a Mayor in its own image. It likes the
policy of take-your-time and all's-well-that-ends-well; it
likes peace and quiet, joke and burlesque. Celluloid
collars and propelling-pencils bared for action; peevish
protests, inordinate ambitions, and compulsory Progress
—all these may extort its respect; but in the end they
leave our village disquieted and recalcitrant.

★   ★   ★

All the same the world is right—fantastic or spiteful as
the Wheel of Destiny may be, it has this advantage—the
Wheel turns.

Through Mont-Paon (who could believe it?) there
once passed a Senator—a distinguished Senator—and the
Mayor was not on the spot. Preceded by a Théophile
wreathed in smiles, the silent politician traversed without
a word the various rooms of our Municipal Building.
The dust upon its Archives, the spiders in its windows, the
cracks in its ceiling, its crazy tables—*Frou-frou—La Garçonne*—all these could wring from him not a syllable,
gesture, or smile, not a tremor of surprise or alarm. The
exultant Théophile continued to discourse without inter-
mission—of the main-beam, which was "his" beam (a
steel girder, and "my doing, Monsieur le Sénateur"); of
"his" electricity (he would get it sure enough in the end);

of his absolute devotion to the public service; of his dominating position in the municipality—("a real power behind the throne, Monsieur le Sénateur").

The Senator neither replied nor moved a feature. His kingdom was not of this world; even Théophile began to feel misgivings and grow a little out of countenance. Finally, escorting the great man back to his car, he summoned up all his forces for one direct attack. Here at Mont-Paon the Republican and Progressive Party received neither sympathy nor support from a reactionary municipality; but no matter—he would do for M. le Sénateur all that man could do, and more; he would astutely manage the Mayor and make him vote the right way ("for you, M. le Sénateur") at the coming election (or rather, re-election it should be) for the Senate; he would pursue a tireless propaganda among the voters and in the newspapers, *all* the newspapers, of the district—so that from now on he could assure M. le Sénateur... Like a large lemur, the politician turned on him a vague and far-away look of weariness, and handed him a visiting-card; then, with a deep sigh, breathed a single question. "Ah, you are *too* kind," stammered Théophile, choking and almost delirious. "Mon dieu, the only thing I can think of would be the Order of the Palm—if you really feel I deserve..."

Two months later there arrived at the Mairie a confidential notice respecting the candidate for decoration. But so confidential were the questions it contained, that only the person concerned could decently reply to them. Duly summoned, Théophile arrived under shadow of dusk—"in the public interest," as he said—to enumerate his surnames, Christian names, and other personal details. Without flag or fountain-pen, stripped of all his insignia, he seemed for the first time a little at a loss. But Théophile is never at a loss for long. With an autocratic gesture he seized the notice and, screwing up his eyes, narrowly per- used it. With occasional nods of approbation, he read it and re-read it; gazed up now and then at the ceiling for enlightenment; smiled at intervals with satisfaction. Now, more than ever, he was Somebody—invulnerable and impregnable—the one Mont-Paonian whom the Re- public delighted to honour. Finally he seized the pen and of his own accord, in a fine and flourishing hand, revealed to Authority his most intimate Christian names and the place of his birth. When it came to "Profession," he hesitated. "Superintendent of Roads?" Would not that be at once too modest—a little compromising—in- opportune? Might it not lead to misunderstanding? For it must be realized, that it was as publicist, journalist, correspondent, that he wished to be decorated; not for his services to the Board of Roads and Public Works; other- wise all the undecorated Superintendents of his depart- ment would be up in arms. (For, you must know, not all Superintendents are decorated—far from it! And jea- lousy, alas, is rife from top to bottom of the ladder.) But when he came to "Academic Distinctions," there he could feel not a moment's hesitation—having gained, at the age of twelve, that Certificate of Study which now hung enshrined at home, between two enlarged photo- graphs of himself; and then he had attained at forty, with

a good place in the list, his rank of Superintendent of
Roads. As for "Literary and Scientific Publications,"
under that head the only difficulty was to know what to
choose. Here I faintly protested...but his lifted finger
reduced me to silence (though it was I who was responsible for filling up the form), as if I had been the lowliest
of his stone-breakers. "*I* know what's what. 'Scientific'
—no, not exactly. I shall merely mention, as 'Literary,'
my chronicle of local events and my political articles.
You know my way of writing from the heart..." Ah
yes, I knew. In one such passage he had exclaimed—
"How, in such a white heat of passion, should the electors
not see red?" And again, denouncing our "faithless
shepherds," with a cry for vengeance he had flung "to the
Hydra of the people all those who brew their venom
beneath the very flagstaff of the Tricolour, behind the very
strains of the *Marseillaise*." But it was at the last item in
the questionnaire that the real fireworks began. With
complete calm he proceeded to elaborate his own eulogy.
"Republican of the good old breed, unshakable in his
convictions and his loyalty to the present régime...
courteous and impartial, moderate and tactful, the one
and only local correspondent of all the reputable press of
the Midi...completely devoted to the rural population
whose interests he serves and whose enlightenment he
pursues to the utmost of his power" (so much for his
poultices, powders, and preachments). "To conclude,
the whole district will applaud the bestowal of a distinction so justly merited." Having re-read and punctuated
this confidential slip, he stamped it with the municipal

stamp, took it up again, contemplated it anew. Was there
nothing he had left out? Ah, he found it hard indeed to
relinquish this new mark of his own greatness. To be
able to handle his own report, glowing with all its
eulogies; and to claim, in the name of his grateful district,
under the official seal, the Order of the Palm! All past
injustices were wiped out; no one could prevent him now,
as the head of Council and village alike, from leading
Mont-Paon along the path of Progress.

On the first of January, no ribbon. Extreme agitation
on the part of Théophile. A letter, respectful, but firm, to
the Senator. "Yes, the Senator knew—was doing his
utmost—pressure on the Minister—it would be in
February or March." Reassured, Théophile spread the
glad tidings among a few colleagues and superiors, inviting them to join him on the happy day in watering his
violet silk ribbon; then ordered by return a case of sparkling wine, "grand crû de Rognac" (which is as good as
champagne, and less expensive). His superior in the
Department of Roads and Bridges replied to his letter
with a rhapsody—"This ribbon that decorates you, will
open for you every door, as well as your virgin button-
hole, which will now flower with the spring." A fellow-
Superintendent wrote in fury: "You may be *recom-
mended*, old fellow, but to get the Palm you'll need a
pretty good pulling of wires. Look out for somebody
who can do that for you; and (believe me as a friend)
you'll have to pull hard!" The rest returned no answer
whatever; for jealousy, alas, is rife from top to bottom of
the ladder.

February passed. The violets flowered, but not the
virgin button-hole of Théophile. He had to wait till the
flowering of the fig and the promotion of a small, dis-
gruntled batch. Still in the end "it" arrived: and one
Sunday, in the bowling-alley, our Superintendent of
Roads displayed his pretty mauve ribbon. But what
happens in a backward locality like ours? "Ah, so you've
got your Order of the Leek!" laughed Pascal, just as he
was throwing the jack. "You've got your Leek—you
who don't even know carrot from parsley! Have to
keep it well watered, won't you, old man!" And that
was all; absolutely all.

Can you wonder, after that, if our road-menders are
worked to death; if savage reports go pouring in to the
Department of Roads and Bridges; if our partisans of the
Left, those traitors to the Republic, find themselves re-
viled with invective hitherto unheard of; if in the hours
when Théophile still persists in delivering letters and
circulars, new sarcasms are vented against garlic and the
herbs growing on our hills? Can you wonder if even in
the bosom of our quiet Municipal Council the leaven of
the Party of Progress ferments more fiercely than ever?
Our dictator is growing exasperated. He wants to "cap-
ture" Mont-Paon; to show it who he is—impose upon it
four, even six, electric lamps, if he is driven to extremities;
in fine, to force a division. And if there is opposition, who
knows?—he is capable of demanding a whole railway
station! "I shall take steps in the proper quarters—you
shall see what I am made of!" The Mayor laughs; but
his laugh rings a little hollow.

God of Justice, who seest so much labour done in vain,
and knowest in Thy omniscience what black worm it is
that gnaws the bosom of our Superintendent; merciless
Deity, that sufferest Science with its powders and its
secrets to be daily outraged by our empiricism; hast Thou
not scourged enough the pride of this Thy creature?
Wilt Thou have no more compassion on sin and anguish?
Wilt Thou not cast down the Council of Mont-Paon
before the flag of Théophile? Ah, for pity's sake, let him
be elected Mayor—unanimously elected—let the law be
overruled, if indeed the law looks askance!

But the Almighty, wearier and more indifferent than
the weariest of Senators, vouchsafes no word, no look, no
sign. He leaves the Mont-Paonnais joining in Pascal's
laughter at Théophile's chocolate medal; and on Section
88, where storms of insubordination rage, He suffers to
be scrawled in charcoal on the trunks of plane-trees, or on
the notice-board of "Work in Progress," this most unjust
distich—

Mont-Paon will never, never have for Mayor
The chief of those that knows what horns they wear!*

* Mont-Paon n'aura jamais pour maire
 Le roi des cornards volontaires!

THE INHERITANCE

To-day the three o'clock post, never large, contained some highly interesting matter: first of all, a catalogue of tombs in every style, of the finest workmanship, giving every comfort and luxury; with the most enticing offers for combined family-arrangements, and ruinous reductions for orders given in advance; next, a sample-packet of the products of the famous brand of the "Black Lion" (figuring also as the "White Lion" in the world of soap); then a free copy of the *Civil Servants' Clarion*; and finally a letter from the *juge de paix* of Briançon. This letter was so extraordinary as to drown at once the clarion-calls alike of the Civil Servants, the Black and White Lions, and the undertakers. Liffran—think of it!—Liffran had come into an inheritance.

It meant waiting on the road that evening for the bleating of his flock, the rattle of his wheelbarrow, the scrape-scrape of his wooden shoes.

He came—with his barrow, his cough, his wooden shoes. A sharp and bitter Tramontane was blowing; his sheep were already safe indoors, chewing at their racks; and Liffran was on his way to buy some bran from the tobacconist—for at Mont-Paon it is the tobacconist that deals in corn and bran, and the grocer who sells tobacco and matches.

"Liffran! Liffran!" No answer. He is too deaf, his cough too bad, his barrow too loud. "Liffran! Liffran!"

When at last I clutch hold of one tail of his woollen cloak, he turns towards me a bearded face nearly hidden under its enormous hood; then, quiet, gentle, cheerful as always—"Hé, bonsoir la compagne!"

"Great news! A letter for you at the Mairie."

"Ah," he smiles slowly, "that *would* be a surprise!"

"You've come into the property of a cousin at Briançon!"

"Ah!" comes the answer, unhurried, unsurprised as ever. "A cousin, you say? Etienne? Dead? Do you know of what?"

Then a long silence. Is Liffran deeply touched, plunged in thought, or simply going to sleep? No knowing. Then with a sudden smile: "You're quite sure it's not a hoax?"

"A hoax by a magistrate! People like that, you know, don't *usually*..."

"Because—let me tell you..." But he does not tell me.

"Anyway, they want you to go to Briançon."

"*That*," he replies, nodding his head from side to side, "must be to pay his creditors! What sort of property do you suppose a poor old devil like me would be going to come into at eighty...?"

"Look here, Liffran, put down your barrow and come indoors a moment; we're freezing here—we'll have an explanation by the fire at our leisure." At this Liffran is as near panic as he is ever capable of coming. Huddling himself more closely in his cloak, he takes one step, then another—"If you don't mind, you'll explain it all another day—by and by. There's no hurry, I can see.

And Bernade'll be waiting for me. Ah, how I *hate* the winter! You've hardly time to turn round—and suddenly it's dark! Yes, yes, I'll be coming round another time, never fear. But, you take my word for it, it's a hoax."

A little later that evening there are voices at my door; enter Bernade, a lively little old woman in a black shawl, dragging after her Liffran in his red frieze cloak and his wooden shoes. It's cold, she remarks—the lamp's very dazzling—she's afraid she's disturbing me—it's black as pitch outside—as for them, they always have their supper as soon as the five o'clock train goes by—and Liffran. . . Meanwhile Liffran does not know what on earth to do with his great cloak—at home he always hangs it on the window-fastening. Ah, that will do perfectly! Now he is quite happy. Bernade too has by now elaborately divested herself of her shawl, then of the flowered neckerchief knotted beneath her chin, and arranged them over the back of a chair; then, smiling under the black butterfly of her Provençal head-dress, and stretching out her hands to the fire, "Well," she ventures casually, "what's this he's been telling me? Coming into property? Is it for certain? Ah, yes, let's hear a bit of it read!" Unfortunately there are in the magistrate's style too many "in consideration whereofs," "eventual collaterals," "prescriptive intervals," "proportions legally reserved" —quite enough to make Bernade's head go round. And yet, when rendered into Provençal, how appetizing is that inventory of the personal and real property of the deceased! The little old woman's wrinkled lips softly out-

line each item in turn; and every now and then the horned
shadow of her headdress on the wall nods emphatic
approval. "Well, Liffran, what do you say to all this
long story?" Liffran has very little to say to it, absorbed
as he is in rearranging the logs on my fire.

"So, if I've rightly understood, he leaves a house all
fitted up, this cousin of yours, a mule, some bits of land—
just mountain, of course, but still!—a flock of sheep—
some ewes in lamb, perhaps, if he knew his job! What
do you think, Liffran? Seems to me he's done well.
Furniture too? And linen? What else? Ah, timber of all
sorts, and sacks of grain...(the rats'll be after those!).
Are you listening, Liffran?"

But Liffran is mumbling his hollow cheeks between his
toothless gums, watching the light ash form flower-like
on the red-hot embers. Suddenly—"Who feeds them,
those beasts?"—he asks in a slow, toneless, far-away
voice, "since Etienne died?"

"Grand dieu! So *that's* what you're bothering your
head about! Why, he must have had some neighbours,
in his part of the world. And then much call you have to
be thinking about their feed at this time of day! But ewes
in lamb!—think how well that would suit you! And
sheets to fit out Jean, now he's coming back from his
military service! Why, for aught we know, the furniture
may do for him too. It wasn't rubbish they used to make,
in *those* days. Look here, you listen to me and talk some
sense. You make me giddy, the way you sit nodding there
from side to side. And don't go on roasting yourself like
that with your nose in the fire, or you'll catch a chill when

you go out. Do you think your tubes aren't wheezy enough as it is?"

Liffran smiles serenely at his wife, but goes on turning over the embers with the end of the tongs; and under the weight of his thoughts his head relapses to its nodding from side to side. Suddenly his eyes encounter on the table the official letter. He stretches out one cautious hand, hesitates, then takes hold of the document, handles it with some apprehension, contemplates for a long while the magisterial hieroglyphs, and then, longer still, the judicial seal, shakes a discouraged head; then, slowly—"Well, if you ask *me*, it's all a hoax."

"But you're as headstrong as a red donkey! You've been told, a dozen times now, that he's *dead*—and dead without children! Use your wits, my dear. You make one's head ache." She ends with a laugh, this quick-tempered Bernade, shaking Liffran by the shoulder as he looks at her—an amused Liffran, grown almost tender.

"He's died without children, do you understand?"

"I understand all right—he wasn't married. Girls—when we were young—why, he hardly even noticed them. So you see—he never felt inclined..."

"No, bon dieu!—he was wise! Look here, to come back to business—no child, no will, and you, Liffran, the only heir. Why, you're in luck's way for once."

"I wonder..."

"You wonder what?"

"If I really am the only relative."

"But the law says so."

"The law says so? But *I* know there's another cousin,

at Cucuron. And *you* know it, too—I told you so at supper."

"Oh!" protests Bernade, suddenly crimson, "you'll get lost on these side-tracks... If there's another cousin, the law will have written to him, never you worry about that...that's the law's business; not ours."

"He had a brother too, had Etienne. The question is, what's become of *him*? Suppose, now, he happened to turn up? We should have to hand everything back. And I'd just have had the expense and the bother and all."

"Well, but he may be dead too. The world won't stop turning just for *him*. And he's only got to come forward; no one's going to do him out of his just rights. All the same, if he *is* dead, do you think you're going to wait for his resurrection? He's been away in foreign parts, since...since when?"

"Oh, who can say? More than sixty years, it must be."

"And never a breath of a whisper of him?"

"Not that I know of. Ah! there's no denying it, the post-office doesn't make much profit out of *our* family."

"Then it's certain; he *must* be dead! He was—you've told me a hundred times over—in that place where they get yellow fever, in—one moment, it's on the tip of my tongue—a name beginning with Blan... Blan..."

"No, not Blan, I've told you a thousand times, in Mala Fesca. Africa way...or America...? It's so long ago, I've rather forgotten."

"Very well, then, is it a country without any post, this Malafosca? Couldn't the man give some sign of life?

Say what he was up to? Whether he was alive or dead? After all, we aren't just so many dumb animals."

"All very well for you to talk, with all the letters *you* ever write!" teases Liffran gently.

"I?—as if I had anything to do with it all! And please remember it's not *my* property. Here's a pretty fuss, to begin with, about a fellow that treated his whole family as a mere joke. The law's only got to look for him. After a certain time, dead or alive, one must just expect to get buried; the world's got to go its way. And as for the cousin at Cucuron, that's simple enough—you just make a friendly bargain with him. You're a shepherd—you keep the sheep; as for him—"

"Now that I think of it—listen—I don't think he *can* claim very much, this cousin, because..."

"Ah, you're waking up, at last."

"Because—you see—he's a bastard. Ah yes!—such is life, one can't have everything one's own way in this world! His father had him by a servant. Dear, dear!— one gets thoughtless at such moments...! He owned to the child—was always talking of making it all right in law —but he put off and put off, as we all of us do, till he caught the cholera. One doesn't think; then something goes and happens...To cut the story short, as far as this property is concerned..."

Bernade explodes. "Oh, let's hear no more of the subject! Much I should have bothered my head about him, if I'd known he was a bastard! Why couldn't you say so at the start, you wool-gatherer! It would be a little too much of a good thing, I must say, if bastards could come into property like anybody else. What'd be the good of having a name of one's own, and a father, and all the other botherations? So he's a bastard, is he? Why on earth couldn't you say so sooner?"

"Bernade," murmurs the old man, shaking his over-burdened head, "what's the good of stirring up the sadness of the world? Hit at mud and it only splashes you; and nobody's any the whiter in the end."

"Well, well, let's leave the mud alone, you're quite right; never mind other people's business, we've enough on our own hands. Now everything's perfectly straight-forward. You go to Briançon..."

"My word, the rate you go at! I'm to set off for Brian-çon, am I?—just round the corner?—two hundred kilo-metres away! If I was young, and if this was June, well and good—I could walk and take my sheep along with me..."

"But, you monster, when for once you're coming into property, you can run to the extravagance of a train!"

"Oh, you—you're ready to manage everything! I'm to go by train, and let myself in for fifty francs, to say the least of it, just for a ticket; then the magistrate...(and how's he to know I'm Liffran, eh?—the magistrate?)—then the hotel, one thing and another...all for an old shack that's dropping to bits, and half a dozen rags!—or for nothing at all, very likely! You may be sure that all the plums'll have been taken already by the neighbours and the law, between them. It's soon seen that you don't know much about their ways. And the cold, Bernade, are you forgetting the cold in the mountains? And you say my tubes are wheezy enough! At my age one's got to consider everything. And when I've thrown away my health and my time and my money, you'll find I have to refuse to take over the property after all—and think myself lucky if I don't have to pay the creditors, or the doctor, into the bargain!"

Bernade bursts into a laugh, striking her forehead: "Very well then, let's stop by our fireside, like the two old sticks we are—but I've an idea! Let's send our sons-in-law. They know how to talk, they'll go into the business and do all the formalities. You can take the sheep for your share; they'll come to an agreement about the rest—the linen, I'm sure, 'll do for Jean (just think of the price linen is now!). What *can* they possibly lose by it?"

"We'll see," concedes Liffran. "Now bedtime, Bernade! We've spent half the night talking about this trumpery. And the sun'll rise just as usual to-morrow, you may be quite sure of that! No hurry about answering the magistrate. I shall want time to think it over. With the law, you've always got to look where you're going. And when I've thought it over, why, then we shall see, we shall see..."

★　　　★　　　★

A fortnight later, second notification from the Magistrate. Two months later, final summons. "This final period of grace elapsed, the next of kin will be regarded as having forfeited his rights and measures will be taken for the legal auction of the real and personal estate of the deceased, leased-out cattle, perishable goods, etc., etc...."

"You *must* send your sons-in-law, Liffran! At least, let's write and ask for a further delay." That stubborn barrow of his flops down on its feet in the road. Liffran coughs, clears his throat, spits on his stiffened hands.

"Well, I must tell you, I've thought about all your reasons. Why all this fuss? Just about a poor man's coming into property? We've always rubbed along till now, on what we've had; brought up a whole family, started the boys, married off the girls, paid all our debts. What more does one ask, at eighty-two?"

"But Bernade..."

"Oh, Bernade's making a great fuss, of course; she's lively, you know, she talks away, she gets excited—but I'm used to all that. It's only a flash in the pan, it'll soon be over. No! Go to Briançon?—or send someone?... just to get—nothing...trouble...expense...! Let it alone, time'll show."

"But the interests of your children...?"

Liffran looks in my face, laying on my arm his old hand with all its weight of years and wisdom. "The interests of my children? Nobody has any interests to be got from this sort of thing!" Then abruptly, as if he were shaking off a burden: "Look here, if you must be told, I know very well what I know, take it from me, about coming into property."

"...?"

"Yes, I remember, when I was little, an uncle of my father's, a poor devil just like me! He lived off the backs of his sheep, as best he could, from one day to the next. Then all at once he came into a property, just like this; and from that moment, do you hear, from that moment he was done for. The property? Mere gas! Why, the law—well you know it—the law has more dodges up its sleeve than a card-sharper. Anyway—he caught a jaundice for the rest of his days; and the end of it was that he went clean off his head. Nothing will ever make me forget it; and it all came from that property—the bother, the forms to fill up..."

"But come, Liffran, the jaundice..."

"The jaundice, dear lady, is like everything else. It can come from getting a lot of bad blood mixed with your bile. Ah, you take my word for it, I've had experience enough of life, it's only education that I haven't had; there's no plague on earth to touch quill-drivers and lawyers! They batten on this poor world like fleas on a dog. And the fellow that gets hold of this booby-trap of a property—*he*'ll be having to get up early in the morning, I can tell you! My poor uncle was right, indeed he was; fleas, downright fleas...just like on dogs...that's what they are! When my children've learnt what life's like, they'll thank me."

The Magistrate at Briançon has never heard another word of Liffran, heir-at-law of the lately deceased...

HILARION AND HIS TRAIN

Mont-Paon has no clock and never will have—let Pascal lament it as much as he likes—for this very simple reason: "Mont-Paon," says the Mayor, "is the only commune in the world without the slightest need for a clock. Every Mont-Paonnais can tell the time by the sun—and then, there's the train..."

Ah yes, our famous local train, that common laughing-stock—"the Crawler," "the Boneshaker," "the Snail's Express," "the Whistling Wheelbarrow!" An invaluable train, for all that. Coming and going all through the day, with perfect good humour and the best intentions, it marks out our hours and lives; crying "Seven o'clock, Sylvestre, take your horses to drink; give your pigs their mash, Rosalie, and let your poultry out!"—"Nine o'clock, time for breakfast!"—"Two o'clock, out with your lunch!"

At once, on that word of command, horses neigh, pigs grunt; Rosalie bustles off about her business, her bonnet-strings streaming out behind; or labourers down their tools and make for the nearest covert, where the great provision-basket and the fat flagon stand waiting in the shade. At noon, while the exhausted peasants lie asleep under the trees, the Crawler lowers its voice and whistles just loud enough to release the children sitting demurely in their schoolroom. But each evening, as it toils for the last time up the steep gradient, snorting at the bit like a horse nearing his stable, it hardly needs to whistle at all; for, in winter, Mont-Paon is by then fast asleep; and in summer everyone is already on the watch for it—everyone hears it and sees it long before it arrives. Here men work not "from the rising to the setting sun," but "from the morning to the evening train"—and how many mattock-strokes that can mean! So at the first far-off glimpse of that corkscrew of steam, the reaper unyokes his beasts, the haymakers plant their forks in the hay, and the lads shoulder up the girls to ride home on the hay-carts with their softly nodding loads. "So the train was early this evening?" growls the crabbed Madame Augustine, who always finds her farm-servants back too soon. And the young madcap who on her way home has dallied too long with her lover by the brook, always pleads the same excuse—"But the train was *so* late!"

On its shoulders all sins are laid; in all life's happenings it plays its part—laughed at, but indispensable. Between two trains, the down and the up, you buy your bread, your beef, your iodine in the next village; you go to your marriage or your infant's christening; to see your doctor, to send a telegram, or to hear a sermon. It is all the train's fault, if old Mother Canne often arrives when vespers are already over; and if the sinners of Mont-Paon leave the confessional so empty, that is because there is no train convenient for contrition, when the day's work is done. The curé of the district treats us as a lot of heretics, apostates, Voltairians—"Ah, my brethren of Mont-Paon!—ah Sylvestre, ah Liffran!"—all because he sees our pews stand vacant, ever since the Crawler raised its fares. Yet if

in some family there's been "trouble," then, whatever
the price of tickets, we leave everything and rush to the
Halt; and while the deceased takes his way feet foremost
in his plumed hearse along the high road, we crowd like
brothers into a democratic third-class carriage, where
everyone tells his tale to pass the time, gazing out at the
tall cypresses defiling past the windows. However slowly
his horse may have walked, at the next town the departed
is already there waiting; unwilling to travel without us
these last few steps of his earthly journey, on a soil already
strange to him.

What a good train it is! With what charming man-
ners! You should see it take its leisurely way along the
thirty kilometres of line that bring it to its junction with
the P.L.M. Here, where it connects with the main line,
the Indian Mail storms past like a whirlwind, its whistles
blowing; gigantic American locomotives make the
ballast sink beneath them and swallow whole cities in their
smoke; white Pullmans add their note of distinction: but
as for the local Crawler, at the passage of these meteors it
may quiver in every window and blink with every lamp
all down its dingy blackened length, but it remains un-
perturbed. Indifferent to the Mail, to the Calais-Brindisi
Express, to all these bepainted trains of world importance,
it goes back in its quiet way to its own shuttle-game of
to-and-fro, for which it was created and brought into this
world.

"What's the time, *patron*?" asks the engine-driver
suddenly of the station-master.

"Voilà, voilà!" And yet the station-master has suspicions of that oxidized turnip of his; he asks the stoker, who consults the station-hand—all their watches are in lamentable disagreement. A picturesque discussion follows; a very rough average is struck; and it is unanimously agreed to go and have one last bock, just across the way—the matter of a mere half-minute. At this point some traveller new to the branch protests? "Ah yes, Monsieur, we shall be starting in a moment; yes, yes, for certain, we shall make up the lost time! We'll just skip the Halt of Mont-Paon. What a song-and-dance to make over a glass of citron-cassis!"

Natives on the other hand never protest, except in fun. The countryman is in no hurry. He can quite understand that before starting a man will want to finish his conversation and, if the sun is too scorching, have one last *bitter à l'eau fraîche*. For the countryman, when for once in a way he does travel, is not going to make a fool of himself! And so this rustic line has never known the disgrace of a book for "Complaints."

Still, however prolonged the drinks all round or the political discussions, a moment comes when, past all expectation, the train shows signs of starting. There is backed on to it an antique Boche locomotive, graciously provided by the Treaty of Versailles. It sends toppling over one another the passengers, parcels, and poultry dispersed through its carriages; lights its oil-lamps; pants, whistles, screams to warn its travellers, amuse the children, and set the dogs barking; chuckles and gurgles through all its valves; puffs its smoke in every nose; recoils, advances, recoils again; and finally goes waddling off, under the fatherly eye of Hilarion.

"Hilarion? Who is Hilarion?"

"What! Who is Hilarion? Ah, you can't come from the Bouches-du-Rhône?"

All along the train, clinging to doors, running-boards, buffers, there crawls an extraordinary figure, made up of a cap with silver braid, pince-nez always mounted for action, a leathern case, and a ticket-clipper. It is Hilarion, who conducts to their appointed ends Boche engine, carriages, luggage-vans, and ourselves. He knows where to marshal rolling-stock, to couple, to uncouple, to shunt. Or rather he would know, were it ever necessary; only it never is. He keeps an eye on travellers' trunks; he does his best to protect the wooden seats against hens' droppings; he assists, lifts, carries, sustains, and packs in his passengers; he shouts to the laggards, hurries them, waits for them, scolds them good-naturedly; coaxes the hunting-dogs who stand barring the carriage-doors with bared teeth; gives out tickets, and gets badly muddled in the process; loses travelling-warrants and loses his temper with his passengers for losing them; then forgives them, smiles at them—"we'll make it all right at the other end"; finally, still hanging in the void, through some window with no glass in it, he will engage in some quite general conversation. He is everywhere at once, is Hilarion; never quite in the right place, but thereabouts, and never far away; always on his last legs, yet always phlegmatic; just on the point of doing something urgent, which all the same can wait. "What a life!" exclaim the profane. But we dwellers at Mont-Paon, knowing where the shoe pinches him, we hold our tongues and avoid gibes at his expense. Certainly when, as he nears our Halt, the worthy

Hilarion knits his suave forehead and sends us thundering past, full steam ahead, then we look small enough. For, alas, this age of merciless civilization, this age of steel and ferro-concrete, has allowed us on our local branch nothing more than a Halt—a wretched little Halt, built of old reeds, where the hornets nest—a poor country Halt without a road, without level-crossing gates, entrance, or station-lamp. Thither, on moonless nights, the traveller must grope his way; there, wrapped in darkness and chilled to the bone, he must signal his miserable presence to the train by lighting on the track a newspaper blown about by gusts of wind. But even these privations would be as nothing; the cold, the dark, the hornets, the bats, the Mistral that wrenches the reed-thatch in handfuls from the roof, the Tramontane that tears off the posters, blue once, with their friendly warning "Beware of the Trains"—all these would be as nothing, if our Halt did not further labour beneath the black hatred, the implacable reprobation of Hilarion.

For miserly Destiny, to crown its miserliness, has planted this hovel of ours at the very bottom of a hollow; so that its ill-calculated gradients, too steep for so weak a train, daily destroy the momentum of the engine, its driver's joy in life, and the traveller's last hopes of reaching the main line. Supposing there are no passengers to set down or take up, all goes well enough. Hilarion gives a good blast on the whistle and, somehow or other, straining at the collar, panting, groaning, staggering, the train ends by clearing the summit. (Ah yes, I know, an official ordinance enjoins him to stop one minute on principle, whether there are any passengers or not. For we are a commune, and to be respected accordingly. But what is the use of talking about ordinances and regulations at Mont-Paon? What is the use of mentioning it to Hilarion and his train, when we know what we do of that accursed gradient? Théophile himself, who made us pass so many resolutions to secure that regulation for a minute's stop—even Théophile has not the face to extort compliance. "The principle is enough for me," says he, "and, except in cases of necessity, I am prepared to let the train pass.")

Unfortunately, when the price of poultry rises at neighbouring markets, it will happen that old Mother Canne, girt with baskets full of eggs, brandishing in her arms whole bundles of cocks and rabbits, mounts guard at the Halt. Impossible to miss seeing her.

"This is where you're up against it," grumbles Hilarion. "Stop, stop! As if we hadn't got to get started again! Devil a bit *she* cares, of course, the old baboon, about the engine, the curve, or our being late! What a curse it is, this poultry! What asses, those engineers!" Or again, on the blackest nights of winter, suddenly there will come flying on to the track one—two—three newspapers in flames—some Mont-Paonnais is spending a night out. Supposing the paper, lighted prematurely, is by this time no more than a glowing will-o'-the-wisp, Hilarion espouses the cause of virtue; he accelerates all his pistons, blows all his whistles, and abandons to the chaste night of the countryside this skirt-hunting scapegrace. But with Pascal, the Machiavelli of the neighbourhood, such tactics are futile. Ten—twenty newspapers if necessary—will go to feed the flames—*Éclair, Humanité, Action Française*, all parties unite in one light-hearted auto-da-fé. The train has nothing for it but to stop. Pascal intends to see the *Revue de Folies* in the next town, to visit Pinder's elephants, to taste all the pleasures of the city. "Stopping's nothing. It's starting. It's then, I tell you, that we're up against it." A jolt, a recoil, a gasp, a leap forwards—"Devil take the Board of Works—and these touring-companies that debauch our countryside—and the whole damned show!" When, after a whole series of jerks, false starts, creakings and groanings, the train has at last surmounted the summit, Hilarion wipes his forehead; pulls forward his silver-braided cap; adjusts on his nose his displaced pince-nez; and, as he tears off a ticket from its rosy counterfoil, "Ah, you good-for-nothing," he growls, "what ducks and drakes you play with your father's money! You make us all late, make us miss our connections, waste your money and your health—why, it's a perfect disgrace!"

But once past Mont-Paon, when he has recovered his philosophy, his serenity, his constitutional calm, then keep Hilarion beside your glassless window-frame and talk to him about his train. He will appreciate that, and tell you all sorts of things. "We're the line," he will say with pride, "that's caused the most questions in the Chamber, the most campaigns in the Press, the most public petitions. No one else has let the Government in for such a series of rows. Well, I'll be honest—we aren't often punctual, and we do miss a pretty lot of connections. But who's to blame for that? The damned fools who laid the line, to begin with; and then the public, that goes gadding about

day and night without rhyme or reason, instead of working or going to bed. And then, I ask you—time, time!—
who on earth can pretend to be always up to time?—
people can talk of nothing else, these days! Eh, mon dieu!
—wherever we're bound for, we shall arrive some day;
and at the journey's end, whether it's long or short, we
shall each get our six shovelfuls of earth on our heads.
Besides, don't you see, trains are like the rest of the world.
Who is there doesn't have his little troubles? In winter,
for example, it'll so happen that the rails get frozen, and
the wheels skate round without being able to get on.
Well, you just have to wait till the frost melts. It's so easy
to have some mishap or other. You run out of water, or
the pressure-gauge won't work—in a word, all sorts of
little nuisances, that all take time. Well, there'll always be
some silly fools to fuss about it—some idiots that just
won't see reason. Ah, la, la! A pretty game it is, serving
the public. But I'm waiting to see how they like it, the
critics, when they're absorbed in the P.L.M. I shall be
retired before we're messed up with that—or else I'd hand
in my ticket and throw up my job—or transfer to the
Camargue Line. Why? Because it's just pure devilment,
is a big line! The employees are mere machines—neither
more nor less—penny-in-the-slot machines, that's what
they are! Do you suppose *their* station-masters would
have a drink with their subordinates! Just a hierarchy—
that's what it is—and they get their bellyful of it. And
always one eye on the chronometer—now it's 'I report
you a minute late'; now it's 'I put you down for a fine—
so much off your pay!' And as for the passengers!—

they become just so many cattle! Do you think *they*'d
wait a minute for them?—or give them a hand with their
baggage? You can just run for it—regulations! bureau-
cracy! red tape!—whistle and away!—and not a half-
penny more for your trouble at the year's end. Life, what!
Whereas on the Camargue Line, what with poachers,
what with smugglers..."

"Still, the main-line trains..."

"Oh, I know what you're going to say—they do start
to time. That's about all that can be said for them. They
start to time, no mistake; but—! They collide, they tele-
scope, they reduce themselves to pulp—and who pays for
the breakages, eh? The passengers—always the passengers!"

"Come, come, Hilarion, you know quite well yourself
how to run off the rails and lie two whole days grovelling
across the track; don't you remember? And as for smashes,
why, there was that car—and then that drunk fellow—"

Methodically Hilarion rubs the two lenses of his pince-
nez and in his blinking eyes there dances a malicious
twinkle. "Oh," says he, with a laugh, "just a limousine,
a few dogs, and a Piedmontese who couldn't carry his
liquor...! But, mark you, nobody was hurt—not even
the drunk man—it only sobered him right off. Good
work that! We're not to blame. And then you want give
and take in life; *we*'re a good-natured lot, we wait for
people, we lend a hand all round, we understand all sorts
of situations. Here on our branch we're just like a family.
Still we are a train, for all that, and once and again we have
to show the public what we *can* do! If it weren't for that,
what wouldn't our critics say?"

THE DRAINAGE BOARD

Let us hear no more, said I to myself, of these stock charges
of the illiteracy of country folk or the frivolity of women
—this learned treatise I am reading to-night shall vindicate
us all at the Judgment Day. "The Temperament," proceeded that erudite work, "is Biological, the Character is
Psychological, the Individuality is Sociological, the Personality is Moral. Now the Biological is subordinated to
the Physical and the Chemical, in so far as the superior
depends on the inferior; to be more precise, the impulses
of Temperament, its make-up, its health depend on its
environment, which is mechanical, physical, and chemical.
As for the Psychological, which Comte has too much
tended to confuse with the Biological, it is intermediate in
all respects between the Biological and the Sociological.
In this way our series finds itself solidly established. Now
—" At this moment a thunder of blows on the door sent
a log crackling into the hearth and shook and overthrew,
like a house of cards, our solidly established series.

By the light of the paraffin-lamp, flaring and fuming in
the draught, I caught a glimpse of hooded cloaks and of
caps with ear-flaps; of a large mantle shaking with its
wearer's cough; and lastly, of a tall, sunburnt individual,
in an overcoat with velvet collar, who assumed a lordly
pose, twirled his moustache, and announced: "We are
the Drainage Board. I am its President. We shall hold our
meeting in the Schoolroom here. And I trust you will not
refuse to act as our Secretary. I'm a new-comer in the

6-2

district, fresh to the job; and so, if you can show me the ropes..." (Alas, all my knowledge of the Drainage Question was limited to a Bonapartist grant, in our Archives, of watches with cylinder-escapements to the bridging-train of the Meuse; but still I could not with any decency lower myself in the eyes of a Board!) "Yes, certainly, that will be quite simple..."

In their homespun and their wooden shoes, the Members gained our Schoolroom of all work, amid a full orchestral accompaniment of stumbling feet and torrential sneezes, a Babel of grumblings and exclamations. Perched on our combined chest-of-drawers and desk the paraffin-lamp tried its hardest at illumination; and on benches too small for them, stiffened legs and velveteen coats did their best to settle down; but in vain. On every side the shadows shifted and danced; the human figures stirred and groaned; and at each movement the worm-eaten wood creaked ominously. Still the pitch of the various conversations, low and whispered at first, grew insensibly louder; soon the shyness had vanished; and in cordial good-humour these Men of Drains were pulling at their pipes, coughing, spitting, laughing, gaily spreading their elbows on the inky desks.

As for the President, he marched up and down the room. Familiar with one member, teasing with another, he still maintained a touch of that reserve suitable to a new-comer, a hint of the superiority he derived from his rich model-farm, his tractors, his latest types of reaper-and-binder, his light lorry in all its flaming newness. When he was giving advice, his face would light up; but when he was merely approving, it kept its shade of reticence.

Before long, losing interest in the conversations round him, he went over to the blackboard and, pivoting on one elbow, described a vast circle in blue chalk, which he then began carefully dividing up, like a rose-window. "All the same," he sighed, "the others are a long time coming."

"If you've anything to say," suggested Sylvestre, "you might as well begin. It's past seven, and I hate breaking my habits. In the ordinary way, I've got in a good long sleep by this time."

"That may be. But I would rather wait for the others; especially Pascal. He's the oldest hand at this, as he was on the last Board; whereas I'm a new-comer in Mont-Paon, and don't know the first thing about your affairs."

Meanwhile in the darkest corner of the room, the cloak of serge was fidgeting this way and that; got its folds all crumpled into a heap; then suddenly cascaded to the ground, carrying an ink-pot with it. In despair, Liffran waved to me for help with an aged hand almost as dark as the shadows he sat among.

"If I'm here at all," he whispered, "it's not that I've come to speak, still less to listen. I'm deaf as a post; and I never could understand written papers. Such things are all very simple for me—'What do I owe you?'—'So much'—'There you are!' And that's done with for the year. No, I've come now...because, well, I want you to write me a note of a word or two to make them let me off the tax on my olive-grove. It's thirty years now since I sold it—yes, to marry off my youngest girl it was—but sure as I've five fingers to this hand, I still go on paying taxes on it. That's what comes of selling to the rich. And yet, you know, it takes money to marry off a girl—linen, wedding-chest...how was I to get all that just off the backs of my sheep? So I said to Bernade—'As Monsieur So-and-so wants our olive-grove...'"

"But it's fantastic," exclaimed the President, who had strolled over to us. "Isn't it the lawyer's business at every sale to make the transfer properly? When one takes on a job, sacré bon dieu, then one should do it! But here everything's allowed to go—how shall I put it?—"

Our financial discussion was interrupted by the arrival of yet another hooded cloak. "Oh, I've not come to stay," said Jean de Jacques. "Let's have your papers and forms to sign, if there are any; I agree to everything with my eyes shut, so long as there's nothing to pay. I've just come to notify the birth of my boy. In the ten days since the squalling brat arrived—"

The President lifted his arms to Heaven. "Ten days! *How* happy-go-lucky you are about here! At Eygalières, where I live, if within forty-eight hours—"

"If it's other people's soup that's burning, never you mind, my lad!" drawled Jean de Jacques; "believe me—there's always time enough to publish one's own follies. When, like me, you've eight or nine offspring on your conscience already, you'll not be in such a hurry to make it known. Come along now, let me sign that Register of Births, and be off. It's getting late. Want to know the date? Oh my goodness, how should I know exactly? Wait a moment!—Wednesday, maybe?—the 3rd?—

unless it was Saturday? Anyway, it was a market-day.
Put the 5th, put the 8th, if it suits your book—much
difference it can make anyway! What!—time of day
too! You're making fun of me. They must be mad.
The time of day! Just think of it! The time of day! Look
here, the pains lasted all night; twelve hours it was, being
born—take whichever you like of the lot. Ah yes, of
course, its Christian name! Only one, eh? One's quite
enough. Only it won't be 'Désiré,' I promise you!
'Nuisance,' maybe!—what do you say to that? Honestly,
I've not made up my mind what to call it. My wife says
'Jules'; after her poor father. My mother-in-law says
'Pierre'; after her brother. As for me, I wanted 'Etienne'
—can't say why. My youngest girl, who's standing god-
mother, wants 'Marcel'—that's more distinguished!
Just picture it!—a clod-hopper called 'Marcel'! Well,
when all's said and done, I'm damned if I care—put down
the name you like best, put them all down, put something
different; whether he's called 'Jean,' 'Pierre,' or 'Toni,'
he'll just be a poor devil like his father and all his forbears
before him. And now that's settled, good-night all! As
for the Board—you get me?—I agree beforehand to
everything; but as for any expenditure—no fear!"

"*What* creatures of custom you are!" sighed the
President.

"Well now," repeated Sylvestre, "suppose you told us
what it is you have on your chest? It's clear enough by
now that the others are just going to leave us in the soup."

"Well, will somebody go and fetch Pascal! He's the
only one that was on the last Board, he can tell us—"

"Don't look for him at his *mas*," interjected an ironical voice. "He's supping at his brother-in-law's. They've made some mayonnaise and garlic and laid a bet who'll eat most snails."

"The swine! He knows we have a meeting and he goes off to eat garlic and mayonnaise—and the hell of a way off!"

From his corner, deep in converse with a shadow, was heard Liffran's monotone—"But to be sure! Without the sun, what would the earth be? Nothing at all! What is it makes the trees grow? The sun! And the blossoms on the trees? The sun! And the beans? The sun! And the tomatoes?—"

"Water!" replied the shadow. Liffran was taken aback. "All the same," he went on, after a long silence, "all the same, without the sun, without warmth, there'd be nothing; not even a creature, not even a blade of grass, not even—"

"What about the Esquimaux?" retorted the President.

"The what?"

"The Esquimaux! The people that live the other side of the earth, at the other end of it, in the eternal snow, with nights six months long and nothing to see by but the Aurora Borealis..."

"Go on, don't pull my leg. You think I was only born yesterday. A night six months long! Get away, you joker!"

"But I assure you, Liffran, there really are Esquimaux, who live without any sun, in huts of snow that never melts and—"

"Ice that never melts! Not even on the fifteenth of August! That would be going one better than at Brian-çon! You didn't realize I came from there, did you, from the country of snow?"

"But I swear to you—"

"And even if it were true? What of it?" interrupted a peevish hood. "What the hell have we to do with such silly devils, anyway?"

Fortunately for the Esquimaux the door opened like a whirlwind. A chant of triumph startled the Members, while their crazy benches cracked beneath them. The lamp flared and smoked cheerfully amid the uproar. Pascal stopped short on the threshold, laughed, then, beating time, entered to a cornet-version of the *Marseillaise*—"Ta ta ta tzan, tzan, tzan, tzan!"

"Ah, so you're digesting them!" cried a jovial voice from the darkness of the background.

The cornet stopped short on a superb false note. "Ah, mon vieux, don't speak of it! I've won my bet, but I've got them inside me—full to the gullet! Two-hundred-and-eighty-three!—not one less! And mayonnaise in proportion! Maybe, moving about inside, they're going to choke me; but what a supper, nom de Dieu, *what* a supper! You asked me to come—bon!—here I am; but, unless you want to be the death of me, just make room for me next the stove and let me digest in peace. Go ahead without me, I'll sign when it's time to go. If I snore a little during the discussion, just nudge me; but, whatever you do, don't wake me up!"

"Look here, Pascal," grumbled the President, "do be

serious for once. We've not come all this way simply to hear you snore."

"I should just like to see what *you*'d look like with three hundred snails inside you!"

"But I want your help. I'm President, but I can't make head or tail of these budget-records. You're on the Municipal Council; you were on the outgoing Drainage Board; a budget's no trouble to you—and as you're the only one..."

"Enough, enough, not a word more! I know about as much of budgets as a dog of vespers. You must be a very simple soul to imagine that we Municipal Councillors understand what goes on at the Mairie! If you only knew how we managed our affairs! It's true, I *was* on the last Board; but I believe it went out of office without ever having met. In fact that's what decided me to belong to the new one. I thought you were a fellow who was equal to anything; but really you don't know your job yet. I shall hold you responsible for my indigestion. And if I do have indigestion, Toine is quite capable of making difficulties about paying up."

"Come now, no more nonsense, how does your Municipal Council vote its budget?"

"Like this. We meet, preferably of a Saturday evening —no, not here, in the kitchen next door. We talk about the rain, the fine weather, the crops—or we talk a little nonsense; we drink a little white wine; and we put a few records on the gramophone—in short, we make an evening of it; and before going, if it's urgent, we sign our names at the foot of the blank page. Next day, or next month, at her leisure, madame here—the Secretary, what!—copies above our names the budget of the previous year. And if you didn't come from Eygalières—a village (begging your pardon) of perfect cuckoos—I mean, if only you were a little more knowing, I shouldn't be having to explain you these very simple dodges at nine o'clock at night, after all that mayonnaise, at the risk of bursting."

Everybody laughed, even Liffran. Only the President furiously gnawed his moustache. "Well, really," said he, "you're a bit too devil-may-care about here! Budgets aren't voted by simply drinking white wine and recopying... No, it's a little too much! Now that I'm appointed, I shall go straightforwardly to work. Things must alter, and alter they shall. Pass me the papers."

"As you please!—but then why disturb *me* this evening? *I* didn't want anything changed."

"What I'm wondering," murmured Sylvestre to himself, "is how much longer are we going to stop here?"

"Had *you* heard," chanted Liffran, "about people that live, so they say, at the other end of the world, so far that the sun never gets—"

"Silence!—come now!—and listen!" shouted the President. "This is becoming farcical."

"We're going to be here all night, that's settled."

"'...given that the administrative account, including full details of operating costs, together with both ordinary and extraordinary expenditure, and both ordinary and extraordinary receipts resulting from the application of the rate of one centime per franc, fixed by the Joint Board

Assembly of such and such a date, and confirmed by the sanction of the Commission for...'"

Liffran and Sylvestre were by now conversing in undertones: "Don't you go thinking that that grey ointment is any certain cure for foot-rot in sheep. Believe me—I've been a shepherd ever since I was born—and I can tell you this. Foot-rot comes whenever the moon and the month get mixed."*

"You think all this is too simple, Liffran? Never mind your sheep. If they've got scab, I'm sorry, go and see the vet; but at the moment we're voting our budget—a far worse business than scab, nom de nom!"

"'...in consideration that, independently of administrative acts for which the Joint Board Assembly has received sanction from the Administrative Council, and of which it has seen the documentary evidence'"—

"What documentary evidence? Where is it?" droned the drowsy voice of Pascal.

"Nobody knows—but wait! Did you come here just to interrupt?"

Highly amused, Pascal reopened one eye: "I've come ...I've come...*you* ought to know what I've come for. As for me, it's a pretty while now that I've been asking myself that very question. But never mind, I'm not

---

* "Quand les lunes se croisent"—a peasant belief which the authoress conjectures to mean, "when the lunar month and the calendar month are at cross-purposes," *e.g.* when the new moon begins on May 17th, so that it becomes difficult to say which moon belongs to which month; the moon being supposed to exert a vital influence on everything.

sorry to be here. This stove burns nicely... Oh, it's
capital!"

"'...in confirmation both of the administrative
account of 1924 and of the last quarter of 1923, in addition
to the supplementary operations "Nil" of the first
quarter of 1925, included on the minute; from all of
which it follows that the figure of the rate for 1926 has
been fixed at...'"

"Oh, don't talk to me of rates," groaned Pascal. It's
more the moment, for me, to talk of brandy. They're
climbing up my throat, the wretched creatures."

"Silence, once for all, I tell you! '...have heard the
President's Report, debated each of the articles herein
mentioned, and agreed to vote as follows the ordinary
budget of the Drainage Board of Mont-Paon for the year
1927: Office-expenses...50 francs.' What," exclaimed
the President, "office-expenses, fifty francs! You can
buy plenty of pencils for that! Say ten, not a sou more!
Now we shall see.

"'Clearing the irrigation-channels of the locality
known as "The Frog-pond"'...? I beg your pardon, but
the Board is *not* responsible for that work. It's the
business of the riverside proprietors, and if they refuse—"

"Beg our pardon as much as you please," said the unseen voice, no longer humorous at all; "if they do refuse,
then, President though you are, what do you think you're
going to do about it? Bring an action against them?"

"Certainly! I bring an action, I win it, and I compel
them, by serving a writ..."

"Nothing of the sort! If you do win, by that time you're reduced to your last shirt and they've not a stitch on their backs. And if you lose, then you've not a stitch left and they're stripped to their shirts..."

At this point Liffran lifted up a calloused and horny forefinger: "Mark my words, lad, never you scratch lawyers where they itch. Richer folk than us have eaten their own eyes out before now, through listening to *their* fairy-tales. Lawyers—I can't put it better—lawyers are just like black flies—they pounce on the nearest piece of dirty pettifogging, like flies on a dunghill."

"Talking of lawyers," interrupted Pascal in a thick voice, "you realize that we still owe fifteen hundred francs to the most celebrated advocate in the district for having lost us, three or four years back, a lawsuit where all the right was on our side?"

"What, fifteen hundred francs!"

"Where are fifteen hundred francs coming from?"

"Damn it, fifteen hundred francs!—a pretty trifle!"

"Fifteen hundred francs for losing a case with all the right on our side!...Just what I was saying!"

"And you were talking of bringing actions, you miserable fellow! That's why we are all *new* members in this show—to pay off their old fifteen hundred francs!"

Liffran had finally understood—"I told you so," said he sententiously. "Flesh-flies, dog-fleas, lice—that's what they are. It reminds me of a case just like it, that happened at home when I was a lad. I had an uncle—"

"Ah no, Liffran! After sheep-scab, here come Briançon and your uncle! We're not concerned with your rela-

tives. We've got to pay—that's the point! But how?—
that's the question!"

"What, pay for other people's breakages!"

"But what am I to do? If only you'd warned me of
that, Pascal, you may take it from me that they'd never
have caught me for this job."

"But *I* was quite ready to be on the new Board!
What is it to us whether the lawyer's paid or
not?"

"Oh, all very well for you—you're not President...
But what about me?"

"Excuse me, friends, I'm going home. I see you'll not
decide anything this evening." Gravely taking his time,
Sylvestre flattened his cap on his head and pulled down
his hood. "But if I'd only known what was on foot, when
you asked me to be on your Board, I should have answered
—'I like straightforward situations, but not old debts, or
nests of lawsuits.'"

"Hear, hear!" echoed the voice of the shadow. "He's
quite right," whispered two other hooded heads. And all
of them began making in the footsteps of Sylvestre for
the door. At once the indifference of Liffran gave way
to signs of anxiety. "Wait for me, Sylvestre, wait—I'll
finish what I was telling you..."

"Shut the door, please! At least!" bellowed the
President. But not a movement from the two hoods. The
great door yawned wide open on the starry night. On its
wind-swept threshold our two Members, hard of hearing
by the grace of God, were now exchanging infallible
remedies against the caterpillar in cabbages. "They say

one should mark the four corners of the field with holy water; but, for myself, I should put more faith in—"

His fists clenched, his eyes raised to the ceiling, the President fell back on forcible measures. With a pressure slow but sure he thrust out Liffran, his caterpillars, and his nostrums; snapped the latch; furiously erased with his elbow the rose-window on the blackboard; then, dusty with blue chalk, dropped discouraged on to the nearest desk. The room was empty; Pascal was drowsing; there was nothing left over which to preside.

"Get up, Pascal, and let's be going. This is all I can propose. For this year we'll get the lawyer to be patient. We might even—who can say?—give him a little on account, by levying a few centimes on every user of the irrigation-system—they'll scream, of course; but let them go to the devil! For the rest, we may as well stick to the figures for last year. Would you undertake that, madame? We'll sign the blank sheets; then you can copy out the figures at your convenience, and sign on behalf of the illiterates present. Then, as soon as the next round of this show is over, I shut up shop!—be President who will! I'll pay my share like the rest; but as to trying to clear up such a tangle...!"

The discussion reached its close, as always, in the kitchen over a glass of *vin cuit*, whilst at Pascal's request Caruso "si ricorda Napoli lontana." When ten struck, the last two Members rose with a simultaneous jump. Ten, in mid-winter, is a quite unearthly hour for Mont-Paon.

By the nearly burnt-out fire, in the now silent room, my learned manual, reopened at random, seemed more discouraging than ever. Ah, why indeed are not country-folk illiterate and women frivolous? "I am only one," said that severe treatise, "for if I am two, both the one and the other of them are still myself; and when I stand outside myself, it is clearer than ever that I am only one; for one of the personalities is I and the other is I. I shall never know that I am other, unless it is this same 'I' that is other... I grasp my self, and grasp it clearly; but really I grasp nothing at all..."

Just what I was going to say. And whoever grasps the Budget of the Drainage Board will find very little to grasp; and the grasp of that poor lawyer, alas, will not close on anything at all.

INSPECTION OF REMOUNTS

When, on receipt of my "General Registration Form"
for the year, I had asked the Mayor what "Horses, Mules,
et cetera" I ought to enter there for the current twelve-
month, he had replied in his habitual way by telling me to
do whatever I liked—or, for greater safety, to recopy the
list which has satisfied this formality during the last
twenty years. For, after all, why bother the owners, and
break into their day's work, just to make them fill up
declaration-papers that nobody on earth would ever
look at? And so in fact the file of Registration Forms,
which had for the last twenty years been nourishing the
rats on the third shelf of our archive-cupboard, all in-
variably showed the same bays, dirty-whites, greys and
dapple-greys, fixed eternally at the same age.

But either one has initiative or one hasn't. Disgusted
with this dull routine, I finally abandoned to the rats the
old file with its lack of originality. With an adventurous
pen I restored to youth various charming old bays, grown
grey in harness; brought up to years of discretion certain
greys which had languished overlong in infancy; killed,
out of kindness, Maurice's poor old hack that has by now
more aches than joints; in short, did my best to repair the
injustices of the Register and of Fate. Why should Guillaume always push his crazy old cart himself? Give him
a little Arab. And then Liffran, Liffran with his ancient
barrow—here is a little donkey (gentle, oh so gentle, and

mouse-coloured) to carry, in bran-new panniers, his new-
born lambs. Having thus done justice, dispossessing one,
exalting and enriching another, by a last brilliant stroke
I raised from the dead that colt of Pascal's who had
perished so tragically in his first flower; then fastened up
with a triple seal the Form for the current year; and
nobody in Mont-Paon gave another thought to "Horses,
Mules, et cetera."

But one evening (it was Midsummer Eve—somebody
must have cast a spell on us) a gendarme, braced up in
every direction with the very best leather, hammered in
the name of the law at our municipal door and, panting
for breath, handed me a yellow telegram—"Official,
confidential, and extremely urgent." (All official telegrams, as everybody knows, are yellow and extremely
urgent—even when they arrive at midnight to ask you
the number of bone-setters, midwives, and mineral-
water merchants in your commune.) Blasée by experience, I smiled as I opened it; but I did not smile long; for
this time—"The draught-animals of Mont-Paon will be
inspected and checked by a Remounts-Commandant.
The local authorities must warn the inhabitants with the
least possible delay, and through the ordinary channel of
fully qualified officials..."

Through the channel of fully qualified officials!
"Children," I said next day at four o'clock amid the din
of the class, "you will kindly visit everybody who owns
any beasts and tell them to bring them here on Thursday
morning, together with whatever they have in the way of
carts, waggons, floats, and barrows."

"And the mules?"

"Ah, yes! It would be the last straw if we forgot the mules!"

"And the colts?"

"As many colts as possible!"

"They'll play the drum?"

"They'll hoist the flag?"

"Dear me, children, it's a more serious matter than that! But you'll see all together at once the cart-teams of the whole country-side—it'll be splendider than the Procession of St Eloi; and, best of all, you'll see a real Commandant!"

"And they'll let us draw him?"

Ah, Pierre, how I envied your peace of mind! To be able, faced with all that splendour of stars and gold braid, to think of anything so frivolous as caricatures!

But the horror of Wednesday night! My gold-braided nightmares surpassed in ghastliness even those of the Quinquennial Census. I dreamt that a pitiless Court Martial sat in perpetuity at the Mairie, under the grin of our snub-nosed Republic. However, cruelly early in the morning, footsteps, trotting hoofs, neighings, kickings, a vast din of wooden shoes, voices, wheels, and children's cries awoke me from my imaginary terrors to plunge me, without hope, into the yet grimmer horrors of reality.

Springs were screaming for want of grease; dog-carts, all smartened to their Sunday best, were lifting their helpless shafts to Heaven. Sylvestre was likewise lifting his hands to Heaven; things had got beyond him. "What next?" his drooping shoulders seemed to cry; and the

fixed smile of Liffran replied, "Though the worst comes
to the worst, my brother, let us see what happens."
Roaming from group to group, Pascal was making fun
of the Army, the horses, and the "et cetera"; then, suddenly extemporizing—"Yes, mon vieux, and it'll all end
in a General Mobilization. All on the active list up to
ninety, and all the hacks, for the front line in the Big
Parade! Do you hear, Liffran!—we shall march past
together, under the Arc de Triomphe of Berlin!" But
Liffran is too deaf, by now, for jest or threat. Besides, his
calm is so solid—so geological, I might almost call it—
that at the news, however sure and positive, of an im-
pending war, earthquake, or inheritance, at the promise
of Immortality itself, he would only answer, with the
same gentle serenity: "Ah!—you don't say so!"

At this moment he was smiling vaguely, at everything,
with his large blackened mouth—at the fresh June morning, at the fantasies of Pascal, at Guillaume's too tubby
horse, at the anxiety of Sylvestre and of the Mayor, at the
one-eyed mule of Jean de Jacques, at poor "Coquette"
whom Maurice, in his reverence for regulations, had
dragged thus far to die, really and truly this time, in the
arms of the Commandant.

However, the animals, having come at last to the end of
their inexhaustible patience and littered the ground with
their whole reserve of droppings, began pulling at their
halters and biting one another out of irritation. The few
curious idlers, their curiosity more than satisfied, showed
signs of departure; and here and there, among the com-
pacter groups, rose anti-militarist protestations. "Just

have a little patience!" pleaded the Mayor, hanging on to
the muzzle of his "Bijou." And the Municipal Council,
rushing as one man to fill the breach, began patting mules
and asses and begging their weaker brethren likewise to
keep calm—"After all, when did anybody ever see the
Army up to time?"

As if to answer this insidious question, at this moment
three horsemen turned the corner of the road and bore
down at full gallop on the Municipality—the Gendarmes!

"Make way, make way!" cried their Corporal.
"Arrange your beasts in alphabetical order, and look
sharp about it! Everything ought to be all ready arranged
by this time—but you're late, as one might expect. The
Registration Book, madame! And a table! Here under
the plane-trees—and a chair, too, for my Commandant!
Quickly now, get a move on!" While the Mayor wedged
up a rickety pedestal-table before the railing of the Municipal Building, the two gendarmes approached me with
a mysterious air, each with a roll of paper in his hand, and
began questioning me, both at once:

"You have not by any chance seen a golf?" said he of
the yellow telegram. But the other interrupted him with
a curt gesture: "Do you know anyone called—let me
see!—called—"

"You may not know what a golf is. It's—"

"Pardon me—anyone called Gouiran, Marius Paul,
said to have been born in these parts and charged with
mutiny, unless—"

"To put it simply, it's a kind of American game, said
to have been lost—"

"Let me finish, will you? Very well, then, this Gouiran is a deserter, but he is said to have died of illness here in Bouches-du-Rhône, or an adjoining Département, so that—"

"Ah! my good fellows, so that's how you get the vehicles in order!" bellowed the Corporal, beside himself.

"It was for that American lady—"

"—who's deserted—"

"What, you're fussing about your own little affairs, your own bloody nonsense, at an Inspection of Remounts!"

Sylvestre turned pale. "What, it's true, is it," he whispered to me, "that things are going badly?" But I had no time to reassure Sylvestre, no time to learn how one plays golf, no time to discover in what adjoining Département—an incredible old boneshaker of a cart, that must have followed both the Napoleons on all their retreats, appeared at the corner of the road, darkening the sky, scaring the children, sending the colts all rearing. An appalling din of old iron and squeaking springs drowned the noise of neighing and kicking, the exclamations of surprise; until with a jerk and a groan this imperial construction stopped short in front of the sardonic Republic. The soldier who was driving it sketched with his whip a military salute; clattered at the risk of his neck down the three steps below his driver's seat; then, clasping to his breast an enormous hunk of bread and with his mouth full, ran to open the door of the carriage with its little blue curtains. A step dropped automatically into place; and there appeared, one after the other, hesitating and feeling

about for a foothold, two enormous legs, whose khaki
puttees were coming undone. Then emerged a comfortable paunch beyond the control of any pair of braces, a
much-stained hussar's dolman adorned with a little strip
of faded ribbon, and finally an enormous head, red, purple, perspiring, bearded, and jovial; surmounted on one
side by a peaked cap, that had got crushed in against the
roof of the vehicle.

"Ouf!" said the Commandant, "what a frowst inside!—phew, phew, phew!—a little air, that does no
harm!—good-day, gendarmes!—nice trees here!—Ah!
Monsieur le Maire! Good, very good!—phew, phew,
phew!—small gathering, eh?—so much the better!—
let's breathe a little, before we set to work! No hurry—
phew, phew, phew!—provided I'm at Fontvieille by
noon, to lunch with the Mayor..."

Respectfully, the gendarmes stood to attention a few
paces off. With eye, moustache, and hand their leader
signalled to the peasants to keep their animals quiet.
"Now, now, gendarmes," said the Commandant, mop-
ping himself, "don't shoot these good people!—get them
into order yourselves, as you know so well how it ought
to be done. One moment, corporal, you take charge of
the refractory ones, the brutes that are skittish, and give
them plenty of room. You will order them forward, one
by one, as madame calls out their names, in the order of
the Register. As for you, you scallywag, you'll check
them. Get the yard-measure."

"You remember, sir," said the orderly, out of countenance, "that this morning it fell off the roof of the carriage."

"Here's a bloody fool goes and loses his yard-measure! Well, be off with you and find me one—and get a move on!"

"...!"

"Have a little initiative, damn it all! Look for something!...you know!...something long enough... why, a cane, for example! Difficult, eh! You can cut notches for the different classes; or, damn it, you can just measure with your hand—no need to be as accurate as all that! Now, be off with you!"

Sylvestre breathed again. The situation did not look so black, after all.

"At the double, now, you good-for-nothing," shouted the Commandant after him. "We're expected at Fontvieille by noon! Or I'll have you hauled, I promise you, for losing government apparatus." Then turning gaily to the Mayor—"Oh, you know, we could get on perfectly well without a measuring-rod at all— these little details don't signify; but I like to develop the soldier's initiative." Then taking the Register—"Now, madame, if you will kindly call Number One—'André, Pierre, Hungarian subject, four feet five'—(What, only four feet five? Not possible!)—'whitey-grey, four-year-old!'" The animal advanced. "Come now, where is he? Well, Corporal? André Pierre! Is the man deaf? Not come yet? Ah, sacré dieu, never in time, these fellows! André Pierre? Never even heard of military punctuality, the rascal!"

"Here, here!" shouted a tiny little man, swaying about on the back of an immense roan horse.

The Commandant collapsed in his chair, chortling with laughter: "Ah, so you're the Hungarian bantam! And the 'whitey-grey horse'! (No, come now, who's made up that colour?) Look here, my good man, there's some mistake—and then, why, it's a dromedary you've got hold of! Twice life-size—if he's a four-year-old, it's the end of the world coming. Now, Corporal, you've been at the riding-school, just have a look at his teeth." Still chuckling, he bent over the Register; then, seeing me turning green—"Oh, some mistake," said he paternally. "We'll put it straight and say no more about it—the next item will be all right, I'm sure."

But the "white mule," which was the next item, unfortunately proved to be a dapple-grey horse, who could hardly lift his mis-shapen hoofs off the ground and was sent back to his stable without further inquiry. Next advanced the donkeys, all as mettlesome as could be; but the French Army took no interest in donkeys—waved them away without a hearing. Then, when the cry was raised for Pascal and his colt, a look of anxious alarm passed over every face. For, alas, the poor brute was dead indeed. In fact it was the only fatality that had occurred in our commune for the last three or four years. "Believe me or not as you like, Commandant," said Pascal, cut to the heart, amid the general hush, "but I marched him up and down for a whole night to try and open his bowels. Devil a breath of wind would there come out of him! And there he was, swelling and swelling, like a balloon. It was terrible! All Mont-Paon is here to bear me out. There we all were round him. Then I said—'Kill or cure, let's try a mallow-enema.' Well, extraordinary it may sound, but the Mayor who was there rubbing the brute's belly can bear me witness—he forced back even the enema!" Liffran was imitating with his head each movement of Pascal. But at the point when the colt forced back his injection, he remained open-mouthed before the fatal syringe, and it was Sylvestre this time that ejaculated— "Well, would you believe it?"

"Then let's strike off the deceased," sighed the Commandant, deeply touched; and then, when Maurice made as to come forward with his "Coquette"—"Here's one, anyway, that's no balloon! It's a shame to keep him on his legs at all!"

"But, Commandant...!"

"'But'—but what! Do you insist on our burying him ourselves? His age, madame?" The Mayor, seeing my embarrassment, tried to come to my help. He searched— (in vain, seeing that I had charitably killed off poor Coquette)—all down the column, ended by finding something, and shouted "Five years!" The Commandant collapsed—"Call it a hundred and let's hear no more about it! Just splendid he'd be for the Heavy Artillery. Come, you joker, you're lucky that I'm on the retired list, or I'd teach you to go pulling our legs."

At this point the Long Stammerer, deeply embarrassed, twisted his hat round and round, opened and shut his mouth several times, then bravely plunged—"M-might we have l-leave," he said, "to d-dismiss the condemned ones, as they've already b-been passed unfit once? My hay's d-dry, and its c-clouding over. If this m-mackerel sky turns to r-rain..."

"What's he mumbling in his beard, this Ostrogoth

here? Certainly you can take away the condemned ones. No need to bring them here at all—surely they told you that?—eh, Monsieur le Maire? Won't you ever understand what's wanted of you? The condemned ones are done with, once for all! You don't suppose, damn it, we're going over it all again! I shall never get to Fontvieille in time for lunch! And now where's that rascal got to in search of his measuring-rod? Whose turn next? Pietru—what is it?—Pietru-ssi-ni! Pietrussini, forward!"

"Ma ché, ma ché, signor, com' è possibile—'Pietrussini'? Sono qui, Signor Commandante, mi chiamo 'Pietroucini'!"

"Never mind, never mind! 'One mule. Put back for further inspection.'"

"Vun mule!!!"

"Twenty-five years old."

"Twenty-five...oh, madame! But what have zey done with ze registro? Sono proprietario, Signor Commandante, ho comprato ze château, anche besides I have a Citroën. Ma vun mule—oh Dio!"

"Who's asking the fellow about Citroëns? Where's your mule? Not so much backchat, see? You understand French?"

"Si, si, ma mi horses sono due belle bestie—vorth many thousand francs—vun for ze land, vun for ze cart, and due altri per ze farm..."

"Oh la la, shut up! Answer the questions you're asked; understand me, eh? Name?"

"Amabile."

"Good! Well, Monsieur Amabile—what's-your-name?—Petrolini..."

"Ma senti, Signor, I am Giuseppe!—Amabile is ze black horse!"

"Oh la la la la! Write it down, somebody! Amabile Pietrolini, just that! Then—Hungarian?"

"How say il Signor Commandante?"

"Stallion, or gelded?"

"Ma—who, Signor?"

"Oh, not you!"

"I should think so indeed!—hey, Madonna! Quando vun has had so many leetle ones as me and Nunziata...! Ma, is it per Amabile, or per Spumante, zat ze question interessa you?"

"Now look here, my good man! How much longer are you going on pulling my leg? You are in the wrong and you permit yourself...This is a pretty business!... Exactly, sir, it was your duty to come and make a declaration at the Mairie. Well, where *is* it? Yet you've been told often enough—isn't that so, Monsieur le Maire, and madame there? But these foreigners—they think they can do what they damned well like! Don't you forget, if you please, that there's a law in France; that you've got to obey it, like everybody else; and that the French government—phew, phew, phew!—is a reality—phew, phew!—that has got to be respected. Why did you not come? Answer me! Supposing I had you summonsed?"

"Ma, milord—"

"Hold your tongue and let the Lord alone! All this about pedros, and mules, and Citroëns...am I expected to understand Italian? And now, thanks to your devil-may-carishness, I'm reduced to entering your animals without even seeing them!"

"Scusi, ma zey are here..."

"What, they're *here*! But—he's terrific, this fellow! Then what the devil were you waiting for? For the Register to be completed without them? Do you think one can go making alterations in it afterwards? Well, if they're here, as you say, you can just take them home again. And, if you'll take my advice, you'll be a little more punctual another time and not try to be quite so clever! It's not your game at all!"

The Mayor shook his head severely. "It's quite true," said he, watching the Lord of the Manor retreating with his horses, "because they make their fortunes here in France, they think they can do just as they like."

Pascal was in ecstasies; "Ah," said he mischievously, "and it's not for want of explanations from you, is it, madame?"

"Oh, you know," said the Commandant in an undertone, laughing to himself, "the things I say... but they need a talking-to now and then!"

In order to shorten the march-past, Pascal, communicating by nods and whispers behind the Mayor's back, had been condemning with a "C" in blue pencil all those in a hurry to get back to their drying hay. I could see him giving right and left the signal to vanish, while we were taken up with the horses of the President of the Drainage Board. We had saved him up till the last, as a special treat. And now, at the conclusion of the proceedings, after receiving the compliments of the Army and the Council, with the smartest of military salutes he turned his horse's head and rode off like a conqueror, swarmed about by urchins and idlers, while the new iron shoes of his stallions rang again.

Left at last by themselves, Sylvestre and Liffran contemplated with rapt attention the masses of droppings that alone remained, and shook their heads thoughtfully. "Well, would you believe it? I never saw so many!" said the shepherd. Sylvestre reflected deep and long; then in a tone of wonder—"Yes, it must be a change for you after the little black olives your sheep make!"

Happy Commandant! All was over; and he had still plenty of time to reach Fontvieille by noon. He clapped the Mayor on the shoulder, calling him "mon ami"; he nudged the backs of the few remaining Councillors; and would have prodded the chests of his gendarmes, if a sudden disquiet had not set his moustache bristling all at once—"But what's become of that rascally orderly? My good Corporal..."

But at that moment the rascally orderly in question emerged from the nearest row of cypresses and came running up at the full stretch of his long legs. In one hand, like St Joseph with the lily, he carried a peeled stick, adorned with a little tuft of leaves. With his other, like the rest of the soldiers, he clasped to his breast a slice of bread and a box of Camembert.

"So here you are, you good-for-nothing blighter!"

Here he was indeed. With his stick at attention, he smiled all over his broad mountaineer's face and, jovial as his chief, nudged him in the ribs—"Begging your pardon, Sir, but while you're waiting for lunch...if you like the look of my cheese...it's just ripe to perfection!"

"Don't try to shuffle out of it! What I'm saying is, when for once in a way you do show a little initiative, a pretty piece of skrimshanking it turns out to be! What were you up to behind those cypresses?"

"I was peeling my stick, sir!" Then suddenly, measuring with his eye our great bird-shaped crag, the Grand-Paon, all white and blue under its tuft of black pines—"Is it true, sir, that it's the end of the Alps here? Good Lord!—that's all I can say!—(not just because I come from the Eastern Pyrenees...) but I'd never have thought the Alps could finish up as little as that! Ah la la, if you'd only seen the Canigou!"

The Mayor was a little piqued.

"It's the same with us in the Ardèche..." broke in the Corporal. But at this point all the gendarmes joined in. They all came from the Ardèche and, believe it or not, the Ardèche's a grand country—very different mountains from these piffling little stone-heaps; and the chestnut-trees..."ah, bon sang de bon sang!"

Fortunately there remained in the prison—that prison so good for mellowing wine—an old bottle, golden-hued under its cake of dust. Lift it against the sun like a monstrance and you could see dancing and dazzling within it drops of pure flame. The Army, the Gendarmerie, the fanatic Ardèche grew suddenly silent. Before this High Mass they bowed. And at the first sip with its bouquet of sorb-apple and flint, farewell the cows, calves, and chestnuts of the Ardèche—farewell, snowy Pyrenees—and thou too wast forgotten, Canigou! The Municipal Council regained once more its confidence and its honour. The Mayor's elation mounted—"Ah, Commandant, if you could only taste my claret from my hill-vines, that I have maturing over there, the other side of the Grand-Paon! With just a touch of frost—you've no idea!— Tavel or Châteauneuf aren't in it!—promise me, all of you, that at next Inspection..."

THE ELECTIONS TO THE CHAMBERS
OF AGRICULTURE

"I wonder what the Prefecture can be up to now!" said Théophile, as he pitched on to my table an envelope a good yard square and stuffed to bursting point. "I may as well just sit down and see what it's all about."

Out of this capacious package poured a torrent of blue leaflets, white leaflets, pink leaflets, inscribed in large letters—"Agriculturists," "Elections," "Chambers of Agriculture"—and consisting of ministerial decisions, admission-forms, pay-sheets, electoral registers, supplementary sheets, and official reports in triplicate—all marked "Extremely urgent."

"We're for it again, my poor Théophile!"

"Oh," said he with dignity, "speak for yourself. Agriculture indeed!—you know well enough I'm a government official and so, for once, I've nothing to do in the matter." Possibly he was expecting a cry of distress from me, or an appeal for help; but as I kept a stiff upper lip (and a very deceptive one it was, too!), facing with unmurmuring stoicism Peasants' Unions and the rest of this mountain of stationery—"Still, all the same," said he, "I'll come and lend you a hand on the election-day. Incognito, of course—still I can't just leave you in the lurch!"

For a week on end, every post brought fresh lists to be filled up, supplementary classifications to be distinguished, corrigenda of the most vital importance to be written in the margin, or addenda to be pinned, sheet upon sheet, to the original return. It is incredible in what orgies of cataloguing a Minister can indulge! Even Théophile admitted feeling lost in it all. I went off to find the Mayor—"How is one to decide if Guillaume comes under Section A? Are we to class as 'a cultivator with capital' a man who merely owns a donkey, or pushes a barrow?"

"Don't rack your brains about that!" said the Mayor. "You'll get your instructions."

Then, having learnt wisdom from my experience with Remounts, I made inquiries of the Sub-Prefect. His reply was some time in coming; but finally he "had the honour to remind me that information as to the propriety of the classification of each individual in his group, and as to the category in which each elector must automatically be placed, would be forthcoming from the declaration devoted to this purpose which each claimant had to fill up himself." Nothing could have been more lucid. And "by the same post" the Sub-Prefect sent yet another bale of blue leaflets.

But not a soul asked for one.

Hoping to make the refractory claimants claim their votes, I made my school-children distribute a handful of sky-blue forms at every house. Alas! the very next morning, innumerable pieces of confetti, paper birds, paper hats, paper boats, paper windmills—of sodden blue, muddy blue, greasy blue, or crumpled blue—blue paper shreds, blue paper wads, blue paper screws—informed me of the one and only category to which belonged, spontaneously and unalterably, the electors of Mont-Paon.

"You'd better classify them as you yourself think best," decided the Mayor.

I thought best not to classify anything at all.

However, after repeated calls to order from head-quarters (first of all, underlined in ordinary government black ink; then in blue pencil—first symptom of Pre-fectural displeasure; and finally doubly underlined in a flaming and menacing red), once more I was forced to fall back on my own imagination and at last sent in the famous lists, filled up and adorned with categories all more or less fanciful, classifications more or less successful, signatures forged systematically, and unimpeachable municipal stamps.

"I told you you'd manage all right!" said the Mayor.

On the eve of the election, by the last post, the anxious zeal of the Sub-Prefect called our attention for a last time to the importance of punctually opening the poll, of forming the electoral bureau in a strictly legal manner, of guarding the voting-urn with jealous but impartial care, in a word, of hedging the ballot-box with an inviolability worthy of the Republic.

The curtains of flowered muslin were drawn from their dusty repose and hooked up in a corner of the Schoolroom. "They'll all be quite visible as they vote, from the knees upward," said the Mayor with a shrug of his shoulders, "but, no matter, people have only to turn their backs!

Your troubles are almost over. To-morrow it'll be my turn to play the clown!"

∗ ∗ ∗

A good hour before the legal zero-hour, the Mayor and Jean de Jacques were pacing up and down the Schoolroom, making sure that the urn was properly closed, pulling at the curtains of the polling-booth to make them meet, testing the pens, shaking the ink-bottles. Laid flat on our combined chest-of-drawers and desk, a green poster, still waiting to be stuck up, summoned the electors to vote for the list of Figuière—"the true champion of the interests of the peasant..." "For," continued the poster, "the hour for which you have been waiting more than a century, has struck at last... Figuière has only one object, to throw open to you new markets, to free you from the crushing weight of import-duties... to secure the happiness and prosperity of your fair land." Unfortunately the Mayor threw his heavy cloak on top of these just pretensions, obliterating at a blow all the promises of Figuière. You will never discover, Electors of Mont-Paon, beneath that stifling extinguisher, what an Ideal you might have voted for!

"What time is it?" yawned Jean de Jacques. In the absence of any municipal clock, we consulted our discordant watches; and, after the fashion of Hilarion, roughly split the difference.

"It's time, and more," groaned the Mayor, "to open the poll, and form our electoral bureau; but that, like whist, needs four of us. And where are we going to get hold of them, those two other voters?"

His breakfast over, Théophile strolled round and drove us from the doorway with the smoke of his first cigarette and the fumes of his first glass of rum—"What did I tell you? Nobody here! You'll never get a soul! They're too backward to care about getting anyone to defend their interests. See?—you can't even make up your electoral bureau. As for me, I'm afraid I can't help you to-day. Government officials can't vote for Chambers of Agriculture. Still, I'll come back incognito when you want someone to put a shoulder to the wheel. Can't leave you in the lurch like this..."

Jean de Jacques had been ramming his pipe, over and over again. Finally, with a nonchalant air, he marched out to glance up the road.

"Poor old man!" whispered the Mayor to me, smiling, "he hopes to hook in a customer or so! He's been fuming all the morning." But the upshot was that after several glances to right and left Jean de Jacques, lowering his head against the wind, was seen hurrying, hurrying, hurrying straight for home.

"The blackguard!" exploded the Mayor. "Now he's gone too and left me in the cart." Then, badly out of temper, he pulled from his pocket the *Petit Provençal*, the *Petit Marseillais*, even the *Petit Méridional*. He did not read them, only looked at the pictures—"Disaster in Florida," "Monseigneur Andrieu," "The tallest Skyscraper in New York," "The smile of Douglas Fairbanks," "The prettiest legs in Paris." He smacked his lips with delight, but then unhappily his glance fell again on that tricoloured urn; the poor man folded away his newspapers, took up the list of electors, and lost himself in contemplating it. He even went further—he read it. Even that! Such is the power of boredom. Then suddenly: "Misery! You've left out two of them—and two tough customers at that! Now we're for it! You just see the fuss they'll make! And suppose they get the election annulled?"

"But, goodness me!—they had only to give in their names. I can't be expected to know by instinct..."

"Of course, of course! They had only to give in their names, one can't know by instinct..."

"They've had forms sent them..."

"Forms?"

"A whole handful of blue forms..."

"Oh, very well then! I shall just say to them: 'You've been specially given forms—white forms—what have you done with them?' And then, why, if they dare to come protesting, I'll send them to the right-about—'No brawling here! You're in the wrong. If you want fuller details, apply to the Secretary who drew up the lists. I've not been there, I know nothing, it's not *my* business to answer you!'"

Still worried, he paced the room with his hands behind his back. Then, after taking several turns, finding himself face to face with me—"I should have done better to fall ill to-day. Idiots that we are!—we all like to be at the helm; and yet when you get the reins in your hands, you do have to pay for it, every now and again! Well, I've got it in the neck this time. A whole good day's work wasted! And all for what? I ask you! Do you believe— you?—in Peasants' Unions? Unions are all the fashion

now-a-days; just like nankeen trousers when I was young.
What earthly good am I doing here? For all that's been
going on, you could perfectly well have managed alone!"
At last, tired of pacing up and down, he perched himself
astride a chair by the stove, poked it, rubbed his eye-
glasses, blew on them and rubbed again, finally spread out
his newspapers, meditated a moment on the most sug-
gestive illustrations, then in an undertone began spelling
out to himself the advertisements: "'Wanted large ass or
small mule'—(Wants an ass to go riding on? That's the
way to see the world!)—'Loulou, come back, all forgiven,
can't live without you'—(Ah, my clever fellow, you'll
get over it long before you get *her* back again!)." Then
he turned to the local news: "'The desperate pair, fastened together by the young man's red woollen belt, had
promised each other marriage. Unable to unite their lot
in this life, they shared death together in the bosom of the
waves'—(Well may they say that there are fully three
dozen different sorts of imbeciles in the world! A famous
idea, to drown oneself, in wintertime, when it's so easy to
elope!)—'Rain has fallen on our lively little township for
forty-eight hours on end. Thunder and downpour
mingled in one deafening tumult. Though still inclined
to be wet, the weather is favourable for sowing.' The
devil of a lot *they* know, at Sénas, what's favourable for
sowing! Why, in these days one's sure of nothing till one
has the money in one's pockets. To begin with, it's
rained at new moon; and in the second place, we may find
ourselves getting into the Forty Days after Candlemas.
They're not so bad as the Forty Days after All Souls; but

they give you weevils and, very often, mildew. Though, to tell the truth, these Forty-Days notions are just like everything else—things have changed a lot; and there are times you feel as if there was nothing left to put faith in at all."

Then, after finishing the papers, "Look here," he said, "there's the nine o'clock train passing!—I'm going out to have a bit to eat. If they don't want to vote, let them stop at home! And if anyone does come, you'll be here. I'll be back in a moment...but you won't be overrun."

Ah, Republic of Universal Suffrage, disillusioned Republic enthroned above our municipal door, poor broken-nosed Republic with your Cap of Liberty slipping off you, here is the sponge of vinegar for you, the crowning outrage —behold your Voting Urn left unguarded to the rage of factions!

It was only towards evening that a noise of wooden shoes brought me running into the Schoolroom. There in the midst of a small group were lamenting the Mayor and a rediscovered Jean de Jacques. Alas, no, not a soul had been to vote—Mont-Paon is really too backward! At last appeared Théophile, shepherding towards the tri-coloured ballot-box a few citizens with some sense of citizenship and organization, collected by him with extreme difficulty. "If I hadn't taken a hand, it's the simple truth, you'd be sealing up the box without a single vote in it!" Thanks to him, here was at least the Long Stammerer...

It was true enough that the Long Stammerer was here —but not, after all, as a voter; merely from curiosity. No,

no!—no making *him* "vo-vote for Figuière, or for Pr-
Prunière, either; a lot of g-g-greedy devils who just
wanted to have a finger in the p-pie, and p-pick the po-
pockets of S-S-Simple Simons!" And then Sylvestre, as
luck would have it, was so hard of hearing, that Zène had
to shout at the top of his voice to explain to him his own
theory—a little simple, but *how* attractive!—of ideal
Chambers of Agriculture.

"Hurry up, will you?" yelled Théophile in fury.
"The poll ought to be closed by this! *We*'ve still got
to draw up our report! The whole thing's farcical!
Quickly, now! One really can't close the voting at
Nil! Oh yes, the Mayor's vote—of course there'll be
that! What a question! Me?—no, I *can't* vote to-day,
I've no say in the matter. So just think!—who else is
there?"

"I understand you quite well," said Zène good-
humouredly. "Nobody's come to vote, so you just
thought you'd buttonhole the three or four stupidest
ones... Never mind, I can't refuse you my vote." And
so, most obligingly, full in the public eye, Zène folded in
four a vote for Figuière, with his new markets and his
repealed duties, thus giving his solitary voice for the
prosperity of our fair land.

"Ah, race of slaves!" growled the District Superintendent, as a few moments later he watched their leisurely
gestures out in the courtyard. "Race of slaves, what do
you deserve? Nothing, nothing at all! I ask myself why
I persist in bothering myself about your interests. What is
it that prevents me throwing you over—reactionaries,

stick-in-the-muds that you are! And much thanks I get for my pains!"

    ★   ★   ★

The next day's papers, instead of the congratulations they owed us, occupied their front pages with a vehement protest—"Odious serpents and foxes have, it appears, duped the electors"—"The indefeasible rights of the agricultural population have once more been trodden underfoot." Well might we all cry in unison with that virtuous organ—"Shame on those who with their tremulous hands have violated and sabotaged such an election!"

And now—alas, three times alas!—with the ten o'clock post came the inevitable yellow poster for the *second* ballot, proclaiming—"To the polling-booths! No abstentions! We want a clean election! Vote next Sunday for the list of true champions of peasant-interests!—the only ones who will open your way to new markets..."

His newspaper in his hand, his eye-glasses fallen from their place, the Mayor shook his old head in discouragement—"Just what I told you! Does one try to take the reins? 'Pay, then! Stump up! Never mind if it's out of your turn!' Here's the whole thing to begin again! Another Sunday wasted! Wasted for me, that is, of course. The others—you've seen how much *they* do!"

Théophile stood choking. Grumbling beneath his breath, he watched the Mayor's receding figure; then suddenly he burst out: "Did you hear him? No, no, this is a little too much! He's terrific! Terrific is what they

all are! What did *he* do yesterday, the Mayor, I should like
to know! Merely put in an attendance—what more?
Nothing whatever! 'You, Théophile, you just manage
the whole thing. You go and beat up the voters!' Even
Agriculture falls on my shoulders! And as for thanks?—
'another day wasted!' No, no, I tell you, I've had enough
of it; enough and to spare! It's no business of mine—they
can just shift for themselves! Then they'll see! Whatever
happens, I wash my hands of it." He stamped, brought
down his fist, gnawed his moustache. Then after a long
pause, with the tone of a victim, the smile of a martyr—
"I always say that," he went on, disillusioned, "but you
can't remake yourself different, when it's your character
to sacrifice yourself, whether or no people show you the
slightest gratitude."

THE BLACK DOG

As nobody showed any sign of getting in or getting out at
the Halt, Hilarion whistled and his train, putting its back
bravely into it, resumed its cheerful waddle. At this point
a carriage-door opened, and a wooden shoe ejected, right
into the middle of a lettuce-field, a lump of squealing
black hair. It was a dog, a lanky sort of greyhound, who
with his pendent ears and bewildered eyes had an air of
dimly asking himself, just like Sylvestre at awkward
moments, "And what have I to do now?" In the ordinary
way, at our municipal deliberations, Sylvestre sides with
the opinion of Pascal, follows him unquestioningly, and
finds it work very well. Similarly, the dog, on this
particular morning, followed the Superintendent of
Roads, who was distributing from door to door notices of
an annihilatory anti-rat-crusade; and the dog too found
it work very well. There is always something to eat in
Mont-Paon, where there accumulate sweepings of immemorial antiquity—sausage-skins and crusts of bread in
the school-yard, refuse and bones outside almost every
doorway, boiled potatoes in the hen-trough at old
Mother Canne's, or fat vermicelli mixed with hard-
boiled egg for the ducklings of Rosalie...And so the
mongrel very quickly understood "what he had to do
now." But Mother Canne, believe me, is not so old as to
let herself be put upon. She speedily suspected that her
trough was being emptied in no normal fashion. She

resolved to keep her eyes open. She did not have to keep
them open long. An unknown dog, of the most objection-
able kind, the kind that is always hungry, soon appeared
trotting in the direction of her potatoes. The old woman
uttered frantic cries, hurled stones, missed the mongrel,
but grazed the cheek of an innocent cyclist and heard
poured out in her direction a quite horrific litany of
invective.

In a tiny *mas* outside the village lives Rosalie. She might
have been seen, at this same period of Mother Canne's
lamentations, shaking a puzzled head over a brood of
skinny little ducklings reduced to little more than large
gaping beaks. "I give them more and more every day,"
she groaned; "well, believe me or not, they eat three
times as much as they should, and yet they're just wasting
visibly away. It beats all! Somebody must have bewitched them!"

Madame Augustine—"the most important proprie-
tress in the district," by her own account, and certainly
much the crossest, "having seen wandering along her
fences an unknown dog without a collar," sent the Mayor
a registered letter, "to warn him of this irregularity,
which might become a public danger"; and to demand
expressly that "he should take all necessary measures."
But the Mayor shrugged his shoulders with a laugh.
"*Her* hide's too thick," said he, "for any dog's teeth.
And then, to tell the truth, she's mad as a hatter already—
an injection from Pasteur is just what she needs!"

The district gendarmerie, "in consequence of repeated
complaints," did indeed on one occasion enjoin us "to

destroy without delay this undesirable animal"; but, as usual, no one lifted a finger and calm once more returned. The dog continued his regular rounds. He even ended by venturing into kitchens; reaping, as might be expected, here a kick and there a morsel, licking dish-bottoms or sneaking scraps...His innocent soul found that life was very good to live and the world well arranged. And yet how, I ask you, should life really be well arranged for one who has not about his neck the regulation collar?

★   ★   ★

Day by day, that gentle time at last drew near which mists the trees with buds of down. Over the ruined chapel of Mont-Paon there drifted once more the yellow bloom of our pine-woods.

Poor little crumbling oratory, what saint was it, full of illusions, who once reared you beside our Roman Road for the repose of the pilgrim and the edification of our unbelieving Mont-Paonnais? On this point history is mute. For a church to excite interest, it has to have at least an ogive, a Roman arch, a Merovingian font, a sacrificial stone...something as small as you like, but still something rather distinguished. The historian will stoop to catacombs of martyrs, to the grotto of Androcles, to the crudest of legends; but not, mon dieu, to the chapel of Mont-Paon—not to these walls of mere unmortared stone, thrown down by the wind and carved by the rain, these few discoloured bricks, this vaulted arch with no church-bell, this altar-stone where the grey lichens bloom! "When you start a religion" (so the guide to the Alys-

camps at Arles always tells his tourists), "when you start a
religion, you cannot be sure whether it will take hold or
not. That is why St Honorat built quite a small church in
the 'Campo Santo d'Arelate'—leaving himself free to
enlarge it later on." So undoubtedly it must have been
the prudent St Honorat who came, after building his
chapel at Arles, to build ours. But he clearly thought it a
very dubious venture. He refused to waste on us naves,
ogives, or flying buttresses. In the most devil-may-care
fashion, with stones from the Alpilles, he built us a tiny
chapel, a mere cottage of God. And never, never has
there been any need to enlarge it. It remains still far too
big for you, O infidels of Mont-Paon! You never open it,
never repair its windows, never replace its tiles. Bats and
swallows live there in the peace of God; Maurice, whose
farm is close by, matures under the altar his white wine
from the mountain; and the black mongrel, jumping in
by the broken window, was long able to devour there
undisturbed the rabbits he had run down, or the chickens
he had stolen from old Mother Canne, and to take his nap
afterwards in the beatitude of a dog on whose conscience
lies no stain. The curé of the district, however, outraged
by our indifference, has taken matters into his own hands;
and one Sunday every year, when the yellow bloom of
our pine-woods drifts down on the ancient tiles, he comes
with his priors, his prioresses, his harmonium, and his
terra-cotta St Honorat, to hold a service and collection
among us, there in the ruined chapel at the foot of the
Grand-Paon in its blue and gold.

But this year, the priest, his priors, his prioresses, his

little Saint and the donkey who drags that wheezy harmonium up the broken stones of the Roman road, all
recoiled in horror as before their eyes there leapt from the
holy place the black and gawky length of an unknown
hound. It was far worse when they went inside. The steps
of the altar were pitifully profaned. Nameless horrors lay
strewn all over the floor. No incense or holy water could
suffice to expel such a pestilence. Before weaving their
garlands or plucking their mystic roses, it proved necessary, amid the protests of clusters of bats blaspheming
shrilly overhead, to spring-clean the Lord's house from
top to bottom.

When the cleaning was over and night had come, the
poor little Saint of clay was left alone there in the centre
of the altar. Deep in the shadow, with the stars shining
through the holes in the roof, on tiptoe in his sandals and
with two fingers in the air, he blessed the bundles of
asparagus, the scattered flowers, the quiet cobwebs, the
birds of darkness, and even the black dog snoring at his
ease on a couch of soft petals. His head bowed beneath his
too solid aureole, he also was plunged in thought. To-
morrow, at the dawn-mass and at the hastily pattered
vespers (all the time that would be left to him by the
Day-and-night Ball and the Grand Bowling Competi-
tion!) he would have once more to undertake—only to
break it afterwards—his annual public engagement to
provide rain, to preserve the vines from hail, the olives
from the black blight, the vegetables from green-fly; once
more he must promise to avert with the raised benison of
his fingers all calamities and cataclysms, all impieties and

blasphemies...Heaven help him, he lived the life of a dog!

"And I live the life of a monk," hiccuped the black mongrel in his repletion. "What a feast of tripe! What ducks' heads! And to-morrow, what roast legs of mutton, jugged rabbits, stuffed turkeys!" For indeed the infidels of this neighbourhood do themselves uncommonly well.

"O Lord!" sighed the Elect of the Most High, stiff in his robes of homespun, his fingers still raised in benediction; "O Lord, Thou knowest it, notwithstanding—that ewes cannot *all* have twins, nor women have *all* the virtues! The lucerne always *will* get the dodder; the vines, alas, some new phylloxera! Your curé always makes these promises, in both our names (just to loosen their purse-strings); but, Lord, even though the Devil lent a hand, neither you nor I (and well you know it!) can work miracles!"

★   ★   ★

However a miracle occurred this very year at Mont-Paon, on a fine Whit-Sunday—Granny Cartelle died. It is in itself extraordinary enough to die, even at ninety, in this fortunate village where, except for Pascal's colt, there has not been a death of any kind for five or six years. But to die of "a varicose vein cauterized too late by an asylum-doctor, so that it goes to your heart and chokes you," as a witness came solemnly to depose at the registry of Births and Deaths—that was something to disconcert even Science itself.

But the Mont-Paonnais, for their part, were not in the least disconcerted. Frankly, they were delighted. To get one's best holiday-clothes out of moth-powder and, on this splendid Whit-Monday, with the church-bells pealing, set off to the neighbouring town by train or bicycle in little gossiping groups; to throw, on arrival, the due handful of earth and a few drops of water on the poor old woman's dust; then end the day with dance or cinema— what greater happiness could there be for simple souls on a fine Whitsuntide? The black dog first followed the bicycles, but they soon left him far behind. However the family of the deceased overtook him in their market-cart; and so he travelled on with the family. What an adventure! And what a lovely town they came to! Full of people in their Sunday best, full of noise and bustle and pealing bells. The mongrel edged his hollow flanks in among the chattering funeral-procession, now between the legs of the horses or those of the choristers; then, under the hangings, into the gloom of the great church; and thence right into the cemetery-enclosure. There he sat himself down with delectation on the freshly dug earth, jumped violently at the opening twang of the "Dies Irae," found a moment's amusement in the first rattling spadefuls, then took to his heels before the holy-water sprinkler, as at the sight of a menacing stick. Next he amused himself by roving about this undiscovered country, like the masterless tyke he was, snuffing here and there with ecstasy at the scent of game.

Finally, as darkness fell, he descended at a venture towards the town and found just by its slaughter-house a banquet past belief. Then for hours and hours he strolled about the streets fast asleep in the light of their winking lamps. But in the morning, as the shops were running up their iron shutters, at the corner of an alley he suddenly found himself face to face with a certain hard-bitten old reactionary, the dread of all dogs for miles around. The old man stared at the mongrel, then exploded angrily. "This is how they do their job, our municipal dog-catchers," he exclaimed, shaking his fist at a new-posted notice of Regulations against Stray Dogs. "That's how we're governed! Placards at every street-corner about curs without muzzles ... hydrophobia - epidemics ... patati-patata! And all the time the dogs go sauntering round the town, perfectly at home; and our dog-catchers —where are they? What are they up to? What are they up to, I ask! Just wetting their whistles with our good money! We may be bitten, we may have to go for treat-ment to Pasteur or the devil—not a damn do they care! Ah, we've got some gay dogs among us, and some good money-grubbers—some fine town-councils and a pretty government!"

But the thunder of a trumpet cut him short. The town-crier turned the corner of the street, planted himself comfortably on his bandy legs, waited till a sufficient crowd had collected, then with a look of satisfaction twisted his moustache, coughed to clear his throat, gave a final flourish of his trumpet for good manners' sake, and began: "By order of Monsieur le Maire, all dogs straying on the public highway will be seized and impounded at the expense of their owners, who will in addition be heavily fined. As for those straying without collar or badge, they will be at once put out of the way by poison or hanging. The authorized personnel will carry out the regulations in question... Ta-ratata-ratata!"

"But look here, my good sir, *you're* 'authorized'—*you* deafen us all day with your music and your regulations—suppose you just begin by catching that black cur there, that's routing up all the refuse—"

"Oh, pardon me!" retorted the crier with dignity, wiping the mouthpiece of his instrument on his sleeve; "pardon me!—I don't care a damn; not a twopenny damn! I'm town-trumpeter, not dog-catcher. And kindly don't confuse the two."

Believe it or not, however, that same day the Sanitary Department took the road—the Sanitary Department, that is to say, two dust-carts, one open, for sweepings, the other screened with hurdles and temporarily devoted, during the hydrophobia-epidemic, to unfortunate stray dogs. Incredible hacks, all skin and bone, drew these ramshackle vehicles, driven by a hilarious old drunkard brandishing a hand-bell. At the sound of this all housewives were supposed to bring out their dust bins, and all dogs to take flight. Both acted accordingly. But—so true it is that none can flee his fate, and sooner or later retribution falls on all unfortunates without badge or muzzle—the black mongrel of Mont-Paon paid no attention to the bell. In all innocence he was busy turning over some perfectly marvellous offal. The old dog-catcher contemplated him with amazement; then roared with laughter and in his drunken voice began singing—"A sweet young thing—it doesn't know...!" Then again he waited a little, giving the dog time to reconsider.

"You'll have asked for it," said he, at last. "Like the look of my dust-cart, do you, eh, you chump? Well then, here goes, poor old chap!"

The dog raised his ingenuous eyes. A hair-lassoo coiled itself about his neck. The town had found him a collar, at last.

INDIGENOUS FAUNA

The indigenous fauna of Mont-Paon—who would believe it?—deeply interests the Central Government. Every year, towards autumn, the Minister sends up a vast "General Register of Statistics," furnished with numerous "supplementary sheets" and full of square-grated sections, like a stable for unruly beasts. Each column is decorated with a number, a heading, and a very general title...a title of the most meticulous, tactless, inquisitorial generality: "Summary of equine, asinine, and other categories," "Bovine live-stock," "Oviculture," "Cuniculture," "Aviculture," "Density per hectare," "Species bred for profit," "Characteristics," "Extent of commercial transactions," "Gross return," "Deficit," "Balance." And so each year, under warrant of the municipal stamp and the signature of the Mayor, I regularly repeat to the Minister (who has never come to check my returns) the figures long ago decided, once for all, by our Council—so many horses and a few donkeys; a liberal allowance of goats; still more pigs; a whole regiment of mixed poultry, laying a fixed number of eggs; and, for all other livestock, a single insignificant flock of sheep. "Profit—nil." "Dealings—nil." "The animals serve exclusively for our personal use"—so our Superintendent of Roads has formulated it.

Thus marshalled in arbitrary numbers in their regular

columns and fastened up with sealing wax, the standardized domestic animals of Mont-Paon go their way
every autumn to swell the ocean of useless statistics. At
first, as a still green official, I used to try to discover what
flesh-and-blood reality lay behind these anonymous
numbered pigeon-holes of our livestock. Fallacious
attempt! In vain I bent above our pigsties. All identically
pink and black, the pigs ate, grunted, ate. Ah, good and
faithful servants, to turn maize and flour, rotten tomatoes
and sour scraps, modestly and mechanically, into bacon,
ham, and sausages!—and then suddenly, on some day of
revelry and butchery, to give it all back again!—is this
what a polytechnic Minister means when he asks for the
"characteristics" of our pigs?

And then our goats—I had great hopes of our goats.
Barren of interest as they might be for the Government,
and barren of profit to us, I still dreamed that they might
display, outside the columns of our Register, that
originality, that gift of fantasy, those "characteristics," in
short, with which they have been credited by literature.
I pictured them skipping along the flanks of the Alpilles;
or hanging, with hoofs poised in the perilous void, from
cascades of clematis; or cropping against the dazzled blue
of the summer sky some flower of cytisus. But in the
Alpilles there is no cytisus; and it is totally untrue that our
goats are in any way madcap, fantastic, lascivious, grace-
ful, or lovers of liberty. The goat of Jean de Jacques,
deformed and dirty, refuses to budge out of its pen and
merely chews dry hay from the horses' manger. The
Mayor's goat is terrified of the wind in the trees. And at

the edge of Sylvestre's meadow, fastened to a willow-trunk by a dog-collar that has rubbed its neck quite bald, there marches round and round, tugging at its tether, a meagre and rheumatic nanny that will not so much as look at a he-goat. Perhaps the kids might show some respect for tradition, were they but allowed to live; but they are sold in tenderest youth to a butcher in Arles, who converts them into "sucking-lamb."

But, as the Mayor says, "one must bow to common sense"; and since the race of goats is thus resigned to be merely a row of brute ciphers on official paper, settled long since by a Municipal Council, why, then, a straw for their personality!—let us record without regret the mistakes we have made.

And then what, frankly, can we expect from the category "Equine et cetera"—from those patient brutes that meet us at every turn, pulling at the plough, marching round our wells, or drawing carts? They offer no interest except, at intervals, to the Army. Though on those occasions, indeed, how the "equine" section of our Register leaps to life! Its motley items come pouring in by every road—shaking the dust from their cardboard files; kicking out with all four feet against the walls of their pigeon-holes; and, with all their "characteristics" in revolt, neighing amorously towards the mares. Grey statistics fly asunder and their fragments solidify into dappled croups, bay backs, fire-red ears, all whirling round the inspecting Commandant in one chaotic saraband—and yet saraband and reincarnation are short-lived indeed! A few moments later and at a wave, a single wave, of that gold-laced hat the whole living paragraph must fatally dissolve and melt away—once more there will be nothing to see throughout our countryside but a few melancholy mares plodding round our wells, a few anonymous horses tugging here and there at cart or plough.

But with our sheep, the little flock of Liffran, it is quite another story. Relegated though they may be by official disdain to the most exiguous section of the Register, filled though their record even there may be with "nil"s, yet these sheared and bleating creatures, of whom Ministers and men of letters expect so little, can show themselves full of both humanity and malice. When the short night of August draws to its pale close, bringing calm at last to nerves long overstrained; when the mosquitoes, finally gorged, fall asleep for a brief armistice; when the labourer's legs forget the ache of their weariness and the baby of the grocer's wife, exhausted with its lamentations, lets the village drowse once more—then the sheep of Liffran emerge from their stall. Bleating in minor thirds, off they go, pattering with their little mincing steps round the dragging feet of their patriarch. They are a mere handful and yet they make noise enough for a thousand. The rams shake their bells and lift up their voices solemnly and long; the ewes reply in chorus, with their mouths all on one side, already stuffed with wheat-straw; and the lambs, for their own amusement, reiterate their childish *tremolos. Piano*, then *rinforzando*, with merciless variations and inexhaustible repetitions, Liffran's flock chants its aubade at each door in turn. It advances three steps, retreats again, bleats while eating, or forgets to eat so as

to bleat the better—then suddenly a *decrescendo* . . . a faint
hope of sleep revives. "Beh! . . . Ba-ah! . . . Baah-ah!"
roars the bell-wether, full-pedal. The whole troop
responds; comes hurrying up, full of anxious enquiry;
takes up the chant; repeats it with all its lungs. "Hey, hey,
Marquise! Fai veni la Negro!" cries Liffran to his collie-
bitch. And when, shaking with fury, Marquise has
fetched up "la Negro," she barks, full of pride and
affection, to get the old man's thanks. But by now "la
Bourrette" has strayed off into the Long Stammerer's
clover—"Hey, hey! Fetch her up, Marquiso!" Every
eyelid in Mont-Paon quivers with weariness and exasperation. Only a single flock, but it is much too much
for such a little village. You meet it on every road;
everyone gets involved with it in turn. While the morning
is young, the harvester perched on his rattling reaping-
machine, the day-labourer already late, the drowsy lad
on his way to market, all find themselves running into the
ewes, maddening the sheep-dog, and themselves choking
with dust while the animals are being got out of the way.
Later on comes the turn of cyclists, car-drivers, and
market-gardeners returning from the town. Peasants may
grumble, drivers lose patience, cyclists protest—but
Liffran is never perturbed. He is far too deaf for anything
ever to trouble him again. He is neither quick nor handy,
maybe, at managing his flock? But, mon dieu, how well
shall *we* manage ours, when we're the wrong side of
eighty? The car is in a hurry? But then Liffran is not.
He has the whole day, the whole year before him; he has
all the little span of life that is left him, to go grazing his

sheep along the roads on the grass that renews itself perpetually. Tranquil and slow, by night and day, he follows
his changeless round across the landscape, only stopping
at noon under an oak to take an old man's brief nap, while
round him his sheep chew the cud, their heads on the
ground, as still as stone. Happy respite of silence, torpor,
repose! Yet brief, alas, for soon the sun will begin to sink
again, waking Liffran and his dog. Higgledy-piggledy,
with their mincing steps and their minor thirds, his tiny
flock will once more go straying up the roads, renibbling
the grass they have already nibbled, exasperating pedes-
trians, holding up vehicles, pretending not to notice the
irritated protests that they raise thick as the dust. But, as
if by magic, just as that dust itself dies down again, so
protest and irritation will die away on the lips of peevish
chauffeur, impatient harvester, rebellious cyclist, or
fuming market-gardener, as, last of all, Liffran comes face
to face with them—Liffran with his tranquil countenance,
his gentle smile—while Marquise—"Hey, hey!"—
fetches up "la Negro."

THE TAX-COLLECTOR'S ROUND

Crusted with dust, sealed with cobwebs, interleaved with scorpions, notched by the saw-teeth of mice, the Cadastral Surveys, Minutes, and Detailed Plans of Holdings lay out on the desks of the all-sufficing Schoolroom waiting for the visit of the Tax-collector on his round of reassessments.

With military punctuality, this worthy functionary arrived a good half hour late, thanks to Hilarion and his train; and his humour had become none the mellower for that—on the contrary!

"A pretty country! A pretty administration!" he grumbled, as he marched in, slapping his leggings with his cane. "Well, is the room ready? Not? Why not? To be done in the Schoolroom, is it now? Ah, sapristi!— one must be surprised at nothing here in the country!" He sighed and cast up to Heaven the look of a martyr crucified—"Well, well! Let's not ask too much. And the Registers?" But at this point he gave a violent start and his mouth twisted into a grimace—"Well, really! Are these what you call 'Registers'? Well, *I* call them 'Refuse!' Passably ignorant of hygiene, eh, aren't you, hereabouts! Poisonous odours in *any* quantity!—much you mind! Don't believe in microbes, eh? Ah, nom d'un chien, very helpful *you* are! And the claimants for reassessment? Where are they? You think, do you, I'm

going to call on them at home? Not a soul here!"
(Sardonic laugh.) "Not a soul!! That's a good one,
that is!"

"I suppose no one's making any claims..."

"Oh, you 'suppose' so? You 'suppose' so, do you?
Nothing like a woman for making such suppositions!
And reassessments—have you any supposition what *they*
are?"

"...!"

"In short, you think them all a joke—that's quite as it
should be. I'm not going to waste time on explanations...
Very good! No claimants, then? Anyway, it's the no-
taries' job to send in their conveyances. You don't know
what I mean? No matter! And the Mayor—is he waiting
for me out there too? All alike, these country people!
What fecklessness! *What* organization! When I was a
captain in the army, I can tell you..."

"Eh? Don't get excited!" called the Mayor, poking
his head under the straw window-blind. "We'll manage
all right, never fear!" Then, settling himself without
ceremony on top of the General Register, he related to us
at length all the bother he had undergone from the rain
last week and the wind this. His almonds were just dropping instead of swelling, his vines had got mildew already,
it was uncertain if the olives would set...he had just left
the water all standing among his fine beans; and while he
was wasting his time here (knowing as much about reassessments as a dog about vespers!), his land might be
getting completely swamped...

"Your beans'll need the less watering, Monsieur le

Maire! Let's get down to serious business. As regards
these reassessments—"

"Oh, you think so! That they'll need the less watering!
And the mildew, may I ask?—do you know how to get
rid of *that*! There can be nothing worse for early vegetables than to get their leaves soaked—"

"No doubt, no doubt, but what I'm saying is—come
to the point!—about these reassessments, Monsieur le
Maire, have you any suggestions to make, any—"

"Oh, my good sir, if you're counting on me, I can tell
you at once you've come to the wrong address. Up to
now you've managed to bleed us for our farming profits
quite fast enough, without any assistance. No need to ask
us for advice! Much you care that the price of nitrate's
doubled, and vegetables only fetching half what they
did! Frankly I wonder—"

The Tax-collector slapped his left legging with fury.
"Always the same story! Will you kindly understand,
my dear sir, that I'm not here to discuss principles, or
rates of agricultural taxation! I'm a Tax-collector—
Col-lect-or—and please don't forget it! I've nothing
whatsoever to do with fixing the tax, or its basis. I am
simply a Collector!—an executive officer—nothing
more!"

"It's more than enough," said the Mayor laughing.
"You skin us, the whole lot of you!—and then you always
pretend it's your neighbour that does it!"

"And if I'm here to-day, its simply and solely to check
the transfers which, in registered sales, . . ."

"Oh, if you're going to try and explain your game of

shove-halfpenny to *me*, I've this very moment told you I can make neither head nor tail of it. So go ahead, go ahead, and some day we'll pay. That's all. Merely a matter of getting used to it!"

"But, bigre de bigre, there's no question now of paying; it's a matter of my copying into the original register—"

"Oh well, if it's only a matter of writing, write away, write away! Why couldn't you say so sooner? Papers—*they*'re all right enough. You sign 'em, seal 'em and say no more about 'em. Go on, I'll stamp anything you like. But, come to think of it, as I'm here, perhaps, if it's not too much trouble, you could give me a trifle of advice... You see—"

"Go ahead, go ahead, Monsieur le Maire! I've something to ask *you* in a moment...let's hear first what I can do for you...with pleasure..."

"Well, it's like this. I should like to buy a little patch of stones that's between the *mas* of my tenant-farmer and the main road. Unfortunately it belongs to the Road, does this particular bit; and the Road, I can tell you, isn't like any ordinary person. The Road-Superintendent says —'It's no business of mine. The Survey doesn't even mark the embankment in question.' And the Surveyor..."

"Washes his hands of it, naturally! Ah, sacré dieu! Look here, my good sir, this is the only course to follow. Consult the Chief Controller of the Department of Roads and Bridges, who will forward your request through the usual channels; or, if you have any means of getting in

touch with him, approach the Chief Engineer direct. Then
have an official measurement made; summon before a
notary the proprietors adjoining the plot in question, for
an inclusive valuation of the area; and have it clearly
specified by your notary that this acquisition of such-and-
such value is to be adjudged you, within its legal delimitations, and with its established servitudes, both passive and
actual, subject to official sanction... You then have the
deed attested by witnesses. That may take some six
months, if you go the right way about it—and there you
are!"

"Yes... because, I mean..." said the Mayor, scratching his head; "what I mean is, it's not worth a great deal,
this strip of ground, it's really..."

"I understand, I understand perfectly, but, never mind,
let's take things in their proper order. You ask me for a
piece of advice—it's not in my line, as a matter of fact, but
I can give it you and I have given it you—and that's that.
Now I've come here to—"

"Yes... but you see... it's full of bushes, and in
future—"

"Yes, yes, of course. But—"

"—one could make a chicken-run there, or a pigsty—"

"Whatever you like, Monsieur le Maire, but meanwhile—"

"—or perhaps even a duckpond."

"Please yourself, please yourself! I say and repeat that,
since the Survey is silent as to the number of the plot—
(damned odd Survey!—must be full of omissions and,

I'm afraid, of errors)—I repeat and assure you, by way of
a friendly turn and just to oblige you, that you must get
out of your notary the essential phrase—'Within its legal
delimitations, with its servitudes acquired and existing,
subject to official sanction.' That, truly, is all. Now let's
get back, at last, to these transfers! Well now, where's
the Register of Boundaries? What, you know nothing
about it! Sacrebleu, what are you thinking of, madame?
Don't you realize that the Register of Boundaries is the
basis—the fundamental basis of everything else? That it
precedes the Road Survey, the Cadastral Survey, the
original Registers...?"

"If it's as old as all that," broke in the Mayor, "the rats
must have finished it, the year of the Great Frost. But—
do you really want it so badly as all that?"

"What a question, Monsieur le Maire!" cried the
Collector, going purple. "I do not, as you say, 'want it
so badly,' since there is neither claimant nor contesting
party, neither sale nor purchase in your commune and,
accordingly, no transfer of property. But, none the less,
the Register of Boundaries being the corner-stone of the
whole edifice, my first care must be to get hold of it, to
consult it, to...for, please understand me, public business
cannot be conducted in this airy fashion, like the affairs of
any peasant. You don't pride yourself exactly on your
book-keeping here, eh? All the same" (he laughed sar-
donically) "it *is* your business. And the General Register?
Where *is* the Register, anyway? No, no, not that one.
No earthly good beginning with the Sectional Register.
The *General* Register! No!—not that filthy object!"

Then suddenly, suffocating—"Now, look at this, Monsieur le Maire, and you too, madame, though the whole matter seems to interest you very mildly! No need to look far, sapristi, to find mistakes—'Number one, Widow Dentu, Section B.' Very well! But the Folio-number? Where is the Folio-number of the Widow Dentu? What do you suppose you can do without the index-number of the folio of this lady? Really, if we are going to have to hunt all through these rag-bags of registers for the index-numbers of every folio!—and to spend our time, when we should be recording transfers, in recopying and correcting...!"

"Widow Dentu?" echoed the Mayor, racking his memory, "what Widow Dentu?" Then suddenly— "Ah!" he exclaimed, radiant, "I've got it! It's the great-aunt of the husband of..."

"Oh, please, please, Monsieur le Maire, no genealogy! No occasion for that, at the moment! Will you have the goodness to send for this Widow Dentu, and make her show you her papers, then have the register corrected and brought up to date, unless you want... It's perfectly inconceivable, such casualness!"

The Mayor burst into a ringing laugh. "Ah, my dear sir, it won't be easy to get hold of *her*, poor old thing! Why, it must be a good forty or fifty years by now that— God knows where!—she's pushing up the grass and daisies. And her heirs? Dead too! Yes, sapristi, all dead, you'll find! What a family! The very thing for you, if it's transfers of property that you were looking for! Two birds with one stone!"

As if jerked by a string, the Collector pounced on the guilty register concerned. "A transfer? You call that a transfer! You have some superb ones, I must say! Ah, pristi de pristi, things go simply here with you! People die without leaving their index-number, they die in eighteen hundred odd, and you expect me, in this year 1927...ah no, it's farcical!"

The Mayor was philosophic. "Oh you know...I only said it to oblige. Here you are, looking for transfers—I show you one—unfortunately it's got blocked there forty years, so I suppose it can well wait a bit longer!"

The Collector grew apoplectic: "But will you understand that, to record a transfer, I must have, first, the deed of conveyance, secondly..."

By good luck at this moment Liffran appeared and the Widow Dentu was left to repose, for further centuries, in the peace of the Elysian Fields. "It's just the same old business," said the shepherd, "these taxes on my olive-grove. I heard monsieur was here... So Bernade's looking after the sheep a moment, while..."

"You've come to pay me, my good man?"

"Ah no, my good sir. That olive-grove has been sold more than thirty years (only think!—since my youngest girl was married!), but the taxes—"

"Ah, so it's sold? And what do you expect me to do about it? Have you the deed of conveyance, for me to make the necessary correction?"

"The...? No—but...the taxes?"

"At last!" said the Mayor under his breath; "perhaps here we have a *real* transfer! You were quite right, Liffran,

to come and claim. It's to monsieur here that one pays the
money; so it must be to *him* one has to apply when one
pays too much—a child could see that! Just as the good
God Himself has always done more for us than His saints."

"Ah, you quite calmly call that 'a transfer,'" grinned
the Collector. "Well, I call it 'a request for abatement!'
And it's absolutely nothing to do with me, into the bargain! There is a Controller of Contributions, to receive
and consider the grievances of complainants against the
Revenue; that's the 'saint' you must address yourself to.
Do you know, my good man, what a Collector *is*?"

"I thought..." stammered Liffran, "any fool could
tell that..."

"Do you *really* know what a Collector *is*?"

"The devil we do!" cried the Mayor. "Certainly we
pay dear enough to know. I'm paying three hundred
francs more this year than last!"

"A Collector collects. Got that? Receives the money
due to the Treasury, the State, the Community—does
that mean anything to you? Employs all the tact, all the
humanity that can be desired; acts as paternally as he can,
gives advice (for nothing, on occasion!); *but*—sacré dieu!
—he *cannot* exceed his powers, nor listen to complaints—
whether more or less justified—nor deal with individual
cases! Understand now, monsieur...Siffran?"

"Then what is it I've got to do?"

"Pay! That's all, without making such a long story
about it!"

"But seeing that he's paying too *much*!" interrupted
the Mayor angrily.

"Pay, and *then* make a claim in the proper quarter. The State isn't a brigand, my good sirs. Make a claim through the proper legal channels; and then consideration will be given, higher up, to the justifiability of your appeal for an abatement. If your reasons are good and well-founded, your money, at some date unspecified, will be refunded. You understand me?"

"Then you want my twenty-five sous?"

"Unless you prefer to bring it to my office! You know my office-days and hours? And in this case, just one word of friendly advice—don't forget that, after the first of next month, you are liable to a fine of ten per cent. for arrears. And don't forget, either, that there are limits to my patience! Paternal, oh, I'm quite ready to be paternal—but only up to a certain point!"

"Well, you see... I've not brought my green form with me. As I was paying too much, I thought—"

"Do you mean to imply, Monsieur Siffran, that you lack confidence in me? No need of your identity-paper in order to pay your debts. To do you a service and save you a visit to my office, I will willingly take your payment here and now. You will receive a receipt by post in due course. We'll manage the whole thing as between friends, eh? When everyone does his bit, everything's so much simpler. Talking of that, Monsieur le Maire, before I go, and as there are no transfers for me to enter, I should like to ask you...if you'd mind increasing—oh, just by a hundred francs or so—the allowance your commune makes me for the visits I pay you twice a year."

"Visits?—how do you mean?"

"For the two visits I make every year to Mont-Paon...
travelling-expenses, don't you understand? If you put it
to your Council, I'm certain they'll understand..."

"Well, we'll see at the next meeting. But this afternoon,
while we've been doing nothing here (and that water's
been alone with my beans!), I've had an idea—I'll put
that to my Council, too—how would it be supposing you
lumped your two visits in one? Mont-Paon doesn't really
want so much red tape. As you were just remarking, it has
no idea of keeping accounts; and I can go so far as to say
this, that one of your visits would really be quite enough
—I promise not to dock a sou off your allowance. You've
given me a piece of advice—very patiently, too!—and
one good turn deserves another! What do you think,
Liffran?"

★   ★   ★

"Well, when all's said and done," remarked Liffran,
after the Collector with his military stride, slapping his
gaiters with his switch, had once more taken the road
towards the railway, "when all's said, what's he come
for?"

"You hadn't gathered? Good!—nor had I! If he only
knew himself!"

"All the same he's squeezed twenty-five sous out of
me!" said Liffran humorously. The silent laughter of his
large blackened mouth, in Liffran's moments of humour,
is strangely touching.

"And just think!" added the Mayor, wagging a sen-
tentious finger, "—you won't believe it—but just think,

Liffran, he's given me, all for nothing, the most splendid tip for my pigsty—or duckpond!"

"Given you a tip?—for your pigsty!"

"That's it. All about delimitations and official sanctions. Ah, you don't understand? No more do I, old man! But I got it all for nothing! As for you—what have you got to grumble about, my friend? For twenty-five sous—a mere song—you've just learnt what a Tax-collector is— and you think it dear! 'I'm a Tax-collector—I collect, whether you owe anything or not—I make you cough it up, on the nail—I threaten you, I blackguard you, and all you've got to do is to thank me for it—and pay me a travelling-allowance into the bargain!' And to talk of an increase, too, for a fellow like that, who's going to mildew my best beans for me! Damn the man! But you wait and see, Liffran—I believe in Justice—I bet you a good dinner, next fourteenth of July they'll be pinning on his coat the Legion of Honour!"

MECHANICALLY-PROPELLED
VEHICLES

"Ah, no," said I to the Mayor who was beginning to adopt a persuasive tone, "don't press me to do that! It's too serious, this time. Lists of electors, lists of the Fauna of Mont-Paon are one thing—say no more about them—but, in these days, 'mechanically-propelled vehicles' are a very different matter! You won't get me this time to do it all out of my own head and concoct whole registers. Supposing nobody, ever, is going to check this one, very well, so much the better!—but in any case it shall be exact, it shall be impeccable! My memory is haunted by that Remounts-Commandant."

The Mayor smiled, as if all this were an excellent joke; his faith remained implicit in the all-powerful force of habit and in that policy of the line of least resistance so dear to Mont-Paon and, indeed, to me.

"I shall stick from now on to the official instructions," I persisted uncompromisingly. "All owners of cars will come here, in person, with their grey cards, their pink forms, their photographs, and the tax-collector's receipt; and after signature by the person concerned, and authority given, their receipts shall be pinned on—"

The Mayor was still smiling. "You mean to say you think they'll come!" said he. "People don't like being disturbed every minute of the day for some form without rhyme or reason—"

"But it's the law!"

"Of course it is, but listen! The election's not far off, and if we rub them up the wrong way too much, we shall end by paying for it ourselves."

"Very well," I replied. "The whole responsibility is yours. But do realize what you're letting yourself in for." And brandishing with a knowing air the special Bulletin of the City of Marseilles with its minute description of the opening of the Station Staircase, "Here" I said, "are the latest decrees. There've been, as you well know, enough frauds, forgeries, and false declarations. From now on you lay yourself open to degradation, supersession, condemnation—"

Deaf to all my "-ions," he slowly filled his pipe. "You said degr—"

"Aï dit," I cried in Provençal, accompanying my words with a continuous dumb-show representing the procedure of the guillotine, "aï dit qu'anarès au tribunau, que pagarès uno bonno 'mendo, et que sarés garça d' esquino!"★

"Bigre!" He stood silent, his thumb motionless on the bowl of his coloured meerschaum. "Bigre de bigre! Well, well, all right, I'll see my people at the café or the bowling-alley, come Sunday, and I'll do my best to make the obstinate ones come. Ah, it won't be easy. But I can't —no, I can't cause you all that trouble."

And in fact, on the official day—if not at the official hour—in the first grey of dawn some unknown wrapped in mist called through my pale window, in a dim, dead

★ "I said that you would be sent before a court, that you would pay a heavy fine, and that you would be deprived of office."

voice—"It's my papers...under the door...if you'll
copy them..." Then at last the sun rose, with a peevish
face, and more peevish still rose also the appointed agent
for motor-registration. Bear thy cross, functionary!—
imbecile, you've asked for it!

Hour by hour, with a monotonous drone of engines,
amid fumes of oil and petrol, arrived the few vehicles of
the commune. Without a murmur I copied out Serial
Numbers, Registration Numbers, Type, Present Condition, Horse Power. The standard Citroën, loaded with
French beans for market, was monotonously followed by
the equally universal overloaded Ford returning thence.
O deadly task! O unknown terms, X of the Insoluble
Equation, letters and symbols past understanding, descended, maybe, from the Grand Key-Word of the
Administrative Enigma, O counterfoils, O stamped
registers and tallies, what file of green cardboard is
destined at last to engulf you, together with all our
troubled slumbers, our wasted hours, our darkened days?
In vain did Monsieur "Apollon," son of "Alcide," get himself involved in a chaos of pompous Christian names and
misplaced information; in vain did the Italian from the
Château introduce into this grey formality the fantastic
note of his own parti-coloured gibberish—these were joys
by now too familiar, surprises too long outworn and
threadbare. Nothing could enliven such tedium. Citroën
followed Ford, dirty cards succeeded to spotted ones,
while the pages of my nauseous register grew full of the
same details, the same melancholy pedigrees of that
eternal 10 H.P. lorry, which, alas, has overrun the world.

I exaggerate? Oh, hardly. And have you not learnt, children of this age, how relative are all things?

Finally that afternoon, a vast Monet-Goyon, all glittering, loudly back-fired, glided easily into the courtyard, and stood there softly gurgling. Airily, smiling, sure of himself as of his car and, as always, in perfect trim, the President of the Drainage Board leapt to earth, stretched out a hand of greeting, then came in to fill up for himself the necessary details and append his signature with magisterial pomp. After so many gloomy faces and dirty cards, fantastic objections and failures to comprehend, stupid comments and soul-destroying figures, as always, the arrival of the President of the Drainage Board brought with it a certain sense of repose—introduced, if I may say so, a breath of purer air. After re-reading his questionnaire with the look of one quite sure to understand it all, and smiling at the intelligence of his own replies, he began turning over the back-pages of the register; he criticized the bad writing on one, the erasures on another; grew witty at each name in turn—despising some and pitying others; pronounced some of their vehicles shabby, and others shoddier still. Clearly they all suffered in his eyes from the capital offence of being low-powered vans of all work. His Monet-Goyon proved the only new car in the list, the only heavy car, the only one, in short, that could be transformed into a smart and comfortable tourer.

But suddenly—"There's still missing from your collection the pearl of the whole countryside" said he with a laugh.

"? ? ?"

"Ah yes! The Stammerer! The Stammerer and his delivery-van! Oh, what a prize that is for Mont-Paon! Ever seen it? Where its paint's peeling off, you can see through it the red blazon of Fraissinet—'Dyers for the World of Elegance.' The very thing for the Stammerer— 'the World of Elegance!' And a delivery-van's just what he wants—a body well closed-in so as to carry inside, where nobody can see or know, his cabbages, his furniture, his pigs on fair-days, his children, his poultry, his manure... Do you remember when he did ambulance for the drunkard that got run over at the level-crossing? For a tip you can make him carry any mortal thing you like! He pays all his rent in kind, and all his stock belongs to his landlord—that's why! I should like to hear him filling up his form!" For a moment, with an absent look, he watched the Stammerer's Black Maria, with its red blazon, receding into the distance on the screen of his imagination; then burst into renewed laughter. "But what I'd like above all to know is the registration-details, the make—the character—the temperament—of Zène's taxi-van! Nom de nom, what a bus! What a super-bus! Since the world became the world and cars have run on roads, never was there such an extraordinary sight as Zène at the steering-wheel! He's everywhere at once, and always broken-down. In the morning, in the market at Arles—in the evening, at Notre Dame du Mal au Ventre—here, in a ditch—there, up a plane-tree—and always looking surprised; above all surprised at the car's going, when by any chance it does go. No matter what happens to him, a burst, a breakdown, a collision, a somersault, he sees it all with the same eyes—dangling his arms he just repeats, 'Coquin de voleur de bonsoir!' I must say I envy you, now you're going to learn the real secret of that phenomenal mock-taxi."

But before that happened, towards evening, I had first to have an absolute single combat with the Long Stammerer. It was a matter, neither more nor less, of extracting from him, in the teeth of his opposition, cards, papers, and receipts. He had flattered himself on Sunday in the bowling-alley, that they "wouldn't catch him this time"; that he'd had enough of our censuses; and that neither Mayor, nor Secretary, nor God's own thunder would make him report again what he chose to keep to himself. If a declaration absolutely must be made, he would sooner go to the neighbouring town. None the less, when his day's work was over, he came to the Mairie. He came, more gloomy, more obstinate, taller, thinner, and stammering worse than ever. "I t-tell you I've h-had en-n-nough of it!" he spluttered across his cigarette-end. "You've r-registered in this t-twelvemonth my h-horses, my wife, my go-goat, my children, my stable...Now it's my mo-motor? Ah, a p-pretty sight of p-papers there've been filled up since y-you've been here! Is it a R-R-Republic we've got, or a Mo-monarchy? I'm not fri-frightened of a woman, and if I've p-paid or not, is nobo-body's business! The th-thunder of God st-strike your p-papers and whoever m-made them! The th-thunder of God...!"

But God did not thunder. The town refused to accept declarations from our householders and, watched by the ironic eye of our Republic, we—we, the representative of the Mayor and Council—had no great difficulty in catching the Long Stammerer and his delivery-van. We triumphed—but only up to a point. When it came to his photograph, there the tide of fortune turned. "You th-think I've the sort of ph-phiz to be ph-photographed! That costs at least six francs f-for f-four. But if you must have my p-papers, you can j-just t-take me yourself, as you've g-got a ca-camera. Each of us d-do his b-bit, hey? I'm qu-quick-tempered, but I'm not b-bad. And if it weren't too much tr-trouble, you c-could t-take my w-wife, too, and our last b-baby, to send to her p-parents!"

On the heels of the Stammerer came Zène—Zène with his tranquil wrinkles, Zène with his hands for ever full of rustic presents. There in the darkness of the corridor he stretched forward simultaneously his face, with its smiling crow's-feet, and two bundles of pink asparagus. Before the paraffin-lamp was alight, he had dumped his present somewhere or other in the friendly shadows and with great haste explained—"Ah, you know, my asparagus isn't going at all well! I've brought them back from the market this morning. These are bruised and their stalks are too short. Not worth tying up—they're just left-overs!"

Zène, who is always giving, has this special delicacy of always disparaging his own presents. His apples? Oh, nothing to speak of! As unsaleable as so much bran or sand! His marrows? The very pigs are turning up their noses at them! His cherries? Oh, but you know,

England won't take them, on the pretext that they have the worm in them. ("As if *we* had put it there! As if it were *our* fault! Pretty friends and allies *they* make!") As for his muscat peaches, that is very simple; if you don't help him eat them, they'll just rot on the tree—a fruit that won't travel, a fruit beneath contempt!

From criticism of asparagus Zène passed to that of the late green peas, which were "going mealy," then of markets in general; blaming these middlemen, who beggar our poor world, and sketching out an ideal Law of Supply and Demand—a little over-simplified and incomplete in its working, an economist might say; but of a kind to disarm all opposition.

However to-day it was not a question of chattering, discoursing, or solving social or economic riddles; whatever the nature of Man, it was for Man to yield place to Horse-Power, statistics, types of car...

"And what about your car, Zène? Your papers?"

He grew troubled and confused; blushed; pushed back from his forehead his enormous black felt hat—a sign of deep emotion; then stammered: "Ah, yes, worst luck, they've just returned my papers to me for the third time—coquin de voleur de bonsoir! Three years running now I've failed in the driving-test! Just can't get it—that certificate! Coquin de voleur..."

I was too touched by this bad news to remember the Register for the moment; loudly I cursed the examining officials, who must have been most unfair; and then delivered one of my most calming discourses. After all, it was nothing so very serious! Better luck next time...

One's not always up to the mark...But Zène, discouraged, shook his head. He smiled still with all his
wrinkles—for he could not help that—but he tugged
nervously at his long Gallic moustache without uttering
a word. I tried everything I could think of to make him
talk, grow angry, vent his exasperation by word and
gesture—no use! Finally, stretching out his hand towards
the bundles of asparagus, as if to call them to witness,
"No!" he said disconsolately, "it's finished, finished,
finished! I'm like that, I am, when they upset me!"

"Finished! The car?..."

"Eh, no! Not the car, worst luck! But their certificate! I'm fed up with it! Let them leave me in peace,
that's all." For, after all, he knows his vehicle all right, and
how to handle it—reversing, putting on the brakes, the
whole contraption...It's just a fatality; the moment an
examiner orders him to carry out the slightest movement,
Zène is completely lost! His forces fail him, his legs shake,
he cannot hear what is said to him, they muddle his head
with a whole stream of French words—and then the tone,
the manner, of that examiner! Ah! what a repellent
being! In short, the day before yesterday, on the main
boulevard at Arles, Zène was just going to take his
corner—very nicely—when the fellow growled something, he thought he was being told to reverse, went
straight about it, and found himself mixed up with a cart
full of lemonade-bottles. You may imagine that after this
disaster he got badly tied up over the Rules of the Road!
No, it can't be helped; but things mechanical, and the
Law—it's not everybody that's made to understand them.

And yet, all the same—(and his hat transferred itself on to his left ear)—all the same there's one's living to earn.

"But, look here, a van isn't bewitched! With a little practice, everybody manages here; even the Long Stammerer. You *must* get your permit, Zène; sooner or later you'll certainly run into the gendarmes!"

"Oh, I've run into them before now! I've even given them lifts (free, of course), not to mention the baskets of white-heart cherries I've taken the Corporal, in season... They're not bad chaps, at bottom. You may not believe me, but they've never asked me to show any papers."

"Don't you count on that!" I put in, full of circumspection.

"I know, I know, they're gendarmes all the same and what's bred in the bone will out in the flesh! But in spite of the whole gendarmerie, I must, I must earn my living!"

"Use your plough-horse to take your vegetables into Arles. After all, not everybody has a car."

"But you don't understand," said he, discouraged, "a hack's no good, now-a-days, for our early-vegetable business. I held out as long as I could; but one's got to keep up with the times. It's not my fault if my land's only good for green-stuff and fruit. It's not my fault if Mont-Paon's so far from the nearest market and life's so difficult. Now-a-days everything has to be up to the minute—if you bring your stuff too late to market, the whole show's over. One's got to go fast; one's got to do like everybody else; one's got—upon my word, with all these machines you don't know which way to turn! Ah, a horse now— you can get on with him. He's obstinate? You just talk to him kindly, or crack your whip. He's ill? You give him a drench. To put it in a word, you know just where you are. But with these machines!—one time it's the carburettor that chokes—that happened to me last week in the middle of la Crau—if you don't believe me, look here at all the mosquito-bites still on me!—another time the petrol-tank leaks and leaves you high and dry, at night for choice, in the middle of the mountains. Or one fine day it's the tyre bursts—and of course your spare one's bound to be punctured too! Or the engine breaks down and there you are—left with your arms hanging, helpless as an eel, in front of your old mangle that won't listen to reason! That was how I came to find myself, on Christmas night, on the road to Sambuc, forty kilometres from any-where—the sort of place where the Devil must have passed the night once, and God, never! It rained, of course, without stopping; and the hood wouldn't go up. I waited, waited, waited; but not a soul to lend you a hand or say—'Hullo, you there, Simple Simon?' Luckily a lorry that'd got lost sent me, next evening, a chauffeur from Saintes to get me going. That's what Progress, and Machines, do for you. And now you want me to..."

A leaden silence descended on us both. Could it be that Zène had really been robbed of all his joy in life...? Then suddenly, "You're exaggerating," I said; "I've seen you myself starting on the pilgrimage to Lumières with half the village in your car—and you didn't look in the least as if you were regretting the donkeys of old days!"

"Ah, that's just where you're wrong," he answered, shaking his head thoughtfully. "Anyone that hasn't seen

the pilgrimages of my young days—all the procession of
carts covered with flowers, the coloured lanterns, the
mules with their pompons—hasn't seen anything. If
you've never been a lover pressed tight up against your
girl, in the dark inside of a waggon that took two days to
do the journey, you don't know about pilgrimages."

"But it's your courting days, my poor Zène, that
you're really regretting!"

"Well, maybe!" said he, surprised and happy. "In
those days all the trees were green; and the leaves have
long been falling now! All the same, folk amused themselves better in my day. If you'd only seen our procession
to St Gens! Thousands of heathen fellows like me wind-
ing up the mountains of Luberon at night, with lighted
candles in their hands, all singing:

> Prouvençau et catouli,
> Nosto fè, nosto fè n'a pas fali…*

But we of Mont-Paon, with Jacques from the Mas du
Diable and the shepherd from the Mas d'Aria, *we* used
to sing:
> Nosto fè, nosto fèdo a fa'n cabré…†

And everybody took it up in chorus. It was a wild success
we had! And next day, at the solemn Mass, when the
priest said 'Ora pro nobis,' the girls would nudge us,
whispering 'Arapo un ome!'‡ Ah, many's the fine
marriage was started in the Saint's Grotto there, and when

* Provençals and Catholics,
  Our faith, our faith has not grown faint.
† Our sheep, our sheep, she's had a kid.
‡ Catch a man!

the women lay down in the Saint's rock-bed, with their heads lower than their heels, to keep themselves from the colic, we used our eyes all right!"

"But what's to stop you now...?"

"Ah, yes! Pretty faces they all are now! Just imagine —last year I took to St Gens our whole Franciscan Sisterhood—old hags that aren't exactly all smiles, you can take my word for it! They made me put on a cord round my waist myself (some stuff about 'getting Indulgences'!) and all the way, instead of 'nosto fèdo a fa'n cabré,' it was just litany after Paternoster, Paternoster after litany. And when we got there, what did we find? A few Seminarists, two or three 'crows,'* a party of devout women—and not one of them would lie down in the Saint's bed or cut the three capers...there's no faith left at all! People don't know how to laugh now! But the worst was still to come. The worst was on the way home. It was black as the pit, in the middle of that Luberon there. Precipices to make you giddy...and then what with tiredness, and hunger, and the time of night, one thing and another, to cut the story short, I went—oh, just while you could wink your eye—I sort of went to sleep at the wheel. Ah, coquin de voleur de bonsoir! It was an elm tree woke me up—and in such a state! You never heard of such a fright, and a shaking, and screaming, and smashing. The radiator was bashed in; Mariette's arm broken; old Mother Canne only got it in the shoulder, but, hurt or not, the whole Sisterhood of them just went for me. What a litany, what a preaching, I got! I promised to have them all put right

* Priests.

by a specialist, and to bring them a basket of pippins—
just smoothed them down as best I could. But think of
the scandal it'd have made, supposing they'd sued me for
damages!"

"They're not such bad-hearted old devils!"

"Oh!" said he, prudently. "Never trust 'em! Old
church-hens, that swallow the good God every Sunday
and wear knotted cords about their middles! What's
bred in the bone..."

"But there's insurance."

"For other folk! Not for me—no fear! Without a
driving-licence I've no right to carry anyone; not even
by way of a kindness!"

"There! You see!" I said, catching opportunity by
the forelock. "You just make another application at
once; and then, with your certificate in your pocket, you
can go and smash all your holy old women to atoms, you
can—"

"No, no!" he groaned in consternation. "That's just
what I came about. Not a word more about it—that Rule
of the Road, and the machinery, and me!...I'd rather
make my own terms with the pious and the police, ill to
deal with though they are! What must be, must. I ask
nothing of anybody—let them damned well leave me in
peace! As for the Register—this is what I wanted to say—
you've just never seen me, you know neither Zène nor
his car, you've never so much as heard of any pilgrimage
or accident. Whatever happens, you lie low. Needs
must, when the devil drives! And now let me finish the
story of my load of old ladies..."

Where are you now, "Mechanically-propelled
Vehicles"? How did you manage to elude the strict
routine of my Return? Your well-ordered series, which
seemed for once to conform so religiously to the Regulations, has grown all faint and shadowy and faded out at
last into the blank canvas of the screen. And that human,
all too human side of our commune, from which it seems
destined never to escape, has gradually risen to obliterate
the whole round of officialdom. What functionary so
case-hardened, what soul so dull, as to be deaf to the appeal
of Zène, this gentle Saint of unbelieving clay bound for
Bethlehem, this smiling pagan with his innocent blasphemies, who recoils in alarm before licences and registers,
who thinks only of earning his bread and reducing to
fragments the elderly devout?

It was a case of silencing one's conscience, and once
more sending in to the Prefect a false return. Ah! guilty
entry left blank!—false virgin, disgracing this fair Register
and pledged to turn a blind eye for ever on Zène with his
disarming simplicity and his unclassable taxi-van...!
My joy, pricked by remorse, was troubled suddenly by a
call, suffocating with asthma—"Conk-k-k, conk-k-k,
conk-k-k!" Could it be the peacock's squawk of the
weathercock above? Or the groaning of the chimney-
cowls, tormented by the wind? Or the hoarse, breathless
lament of some suffering soul on its path to Purgatory?

"Conk-k-k, conk-k-k!" What was to be done?—
cross oneself?—spit?—throw some holy water?—or bolt
the door?—"Conk-k-k, conk-k-k..." it was a horn; but
a most ancient horn, forgotten by all searchers of antiquity,

the Fairy Carabosse of horns, sick, shaky, expiring. Then
the door opened and a figure wrapped in shadow, phan-
tom-like, breathless, appeared in the aperture.

"The Register of Cars—k-k-k?"

"Gone!"

"Gone—k-k-k!" The man in overalls lifted heaven-
ward long arms of despair.

"Excuse me, but...do you belong to this commune?"

"No, I'm only here for the summer, staying. A Tourist,
what! I ought to have—k-k-k—" again he raised his two
arms to heaven; and slowly began retreating into the
misty vapours of the cold May-night. I took up the lamp
to escort this phantom-tourist back into the night, the fog,
the unknown. Suddenly, beside the ditch of the roadway,
the lamplight fell on the most astonishing, the most incredible, the most extravagant of "mechanically-propelled vehicles." At once there leapt to my mind the
confidential question, the delicate question, the only one
that really interests the Ministry of War—"Possible
serviceability in case of mobilization." Alas, this one
"purely touring" car that chance had brought into the
possession of Mont-Paon, proved recalcitrant—not by
any deliberate malice—but absolutely recalcitrant to all
formulas, to the Army, and to its country. Its kingdom
was not of this world. The Minister, who has foreseen,
labelled, and numbered everything, can by one stroke of
his pen automatically commandeer all vehicles "de luxe"
for the "Service of the General Staff." But in practice?—
this vehicle, which trembled in the lamplight with its dark
patches of shadow, shifting edges of blackness, pallid

gleams—it was not fit to carry so much as a troubled soul on the road to Purgatory! Not the most exacting of Ministers, the most cunning of questionnaires, the most zealous of functionaries—nothing, nobody—could ever command its services.

Once more where are you, "Mechanically-propelled Vehicles" of Mont-Paon? Standardized series, exact types, noble list that I maligned, how is one to classify spectre-cars? Alas, for the duty perfectly performed, the ideal Return, that I nursed the dream of in the grey of dawn— here is the ungraspable nettle, the impossible task, the defeat of all my official zeal!

"What make?" I asked, for the sake of saying something.

"Zebra," said the man, unblenching.

Amid the cold white cotton-wool of the fog, which rounded off the beginning and the end of all about us, the Zebra—since Zebra it was—gasped miserably. Giddy, already collapsing earthward at the front end of its chassis, buckled, rusty, filthy, clutching at its balance on wheels too spindly for it, it seemed like some prehistoric animal, bending on its knees to lie down, to sleep, and if possible, to die. Yes, to sleep!—to die! But even so its oilless joints had failed it half-way. Shaken by spasms, rigid on its gouty limbs, it presented the agonized incoherence of a nightmare. Even its lights were failing from exhaustion. Only at the back there still winked a red lamp which, according to the law, should reveal legibly— but no, all had vanished, paint and number alike, under layers of mud, of every age and every soil. The red clay of

la Crau mingled with the grey earth of the plain; the
black peat of the marshes was spotted over with a leprosy
of lime; and its latest splotches, the sodden ochre of
to-night, now dyed red and green by a rainbow of oil,
clung in heavy clusters to the exhaust. So on their
stiffened knees sink earthward creatures overcome with
years, to die at last.

The man tried to galvanize his mount. Another swing
of the crank, a last effort from the engine; it gurgled,
rattled, then gave up. Then the tourist had an idea:
"To-morrow I'll have her towed. Meanwhile, there is,
isn't there, someone in the neighbourhood who does taxi
with his van, when wanted...? Someone called...?"

"Zène?"

"Zène. That's it. He can take me home in five
sec—"

I grew alarmed. "If you'll take my advice, you'll ask
Pascal—just over there—to harness his Arab mule. It's
a most fiery animal, and Pascal will be delighted—"

"Oh," said the tourist, smiling disdainfully, "no, no!
When one's once tasted cars...got bitten with speed...
why, colts, mules, old screws of that sort... Oh, you
know, one would just die of impatience!"

So it came about that, on a cold, foggy night, Zène
found himself broken down in the middle of our olive-
groves, through having, without a permit, out of pure
goodness of heart, given an illegal lift to a sports-loving
spectre.

And so it is, too, that our "Register of Mechanically-
propelled Vehicles," with humanity breaking into it

as into all our other Registers, by the common destiny of
everything at Mont-Paon, reposes in the Minister's green-
cardboard files, blemished like its fellows with errors and
omissions, between the charming scapegrace Horses of
our village, and those humorists, our Sheep.

THE FREE COMMUNE OF MONT-PAON

Yes, no doubt, the hay could not wait—it was the day of days for haymaking; no doubt the rain, at other times so perpetually prayed for, and so unwilling to oblige, always does threaten when the hay is just ready. All the same, what was the Council dreaming of to-day? How could the Party of Progress leave me—with no authority, with no defence—to the wrath of the Engineer—the Chief Engineer of the Rural Board of Works? Could they have hoped, as I did, that this formidable functionary would be daunted by the weather? But when the Devil lends a hand, nothing can stop a Chief Engineer.

In the middle of the play-hour, while I was presiding over "The Grand Bullfight to the Death" which my urchins had just staged, an enormous limousine drew up, snorting like a Boanerges, at our very doorstep. The matadors let fall their wooden swords; their gorgeous mantles turned back again into curtains of faded muslin; and our dead bulls came to life as a brood of childish figures huddled shyly round me, a lamentable Mayor's Secretary, left in the lurch by her Municipal Council.

The boys dashed off post-haste to try to collect some of the Members; the girls, little gossips, began to whisper and laugh at the portly Engineer with his decorations, at his bilious-looking secretary, at their bulging portfolio, at my embarrassed Secretaryship.

Back came the first bicycles—of course they had drawn

a blank. "Pierre at the Mas du Diable has no time—the storm-cloud's coming closer"—"Liffran's rounding up his sheep under the Grand-Paon"—"As for Sylvestre, he agrees to whatever you do"...The Engineer shook his head and laughed. (It looked as if there might be just a chance of coming to an understanding with the man!) The Secretary drummed furiously on his portfolio, and stared in the worst of humours at the hail-cloud, which really was moving up the valley of the Rhone. At the wheel of the official car a most stylish chauffeur sat in complete indifference to everything about him, whistling the same tune over and over, or puffing a cigarette with perfect philosophy. What a situation!

To gain time, and leave the latest loiterers a final chance, I begged my visitors to come indoors, and drink something—indeed I was ready to make any concession, ready to play them my gramophone-records, especially Pascal's favourite Caruso. ("Rather irregular," our Superintendent of Roads would have said, "still one must bow to circumstances.") The Secretary's face was grimly set; this Provençal rusticity, on top of the happy-go-lucky methods of our Council, was too much for him to swallow in one day. But the Engineer seemed ready to take his adventure in the right spirit. He liked our white wine— the white wine we found so useful on Inspection Days; he liked our iron furniture; he liked dogs such as ours—more philosophic even than our Municipal Council, and quite determined not to rise to their feet even to welcome a decorated official.

Excellent man! He forgot, with the best possible grace,

that he was here to thunder in our ears; to demand the plan which our culpable negligence had sat upon for over two years now; to require of us full minutes of all our discussions on this topic of electric lighting; to settle the whole question with one final word, that should decide for ever the triumph of Light, or of Error; and, finally, to extract payment for that map of our commune in blue and black ink, colour-washed so delicate a tint. But he forgot all about his mission; blowing smoke-rings with his cigar, he spoke, not of wires or transformers, of debts or cash, but of the quiet loveliness of the countryside, of the honeysuckle blossoming on the hedges, of his native Nîmes, of bull-fights, of the rights of the Midi... Had he but been slimmer and a sous-préfet, he would certainly have broken into verse.

"Yes, Mistral was right—'Death, or the Revolution!' —for I believe, when all is said and done, that the peoples are free..." Amid this lyric rhapsody arrived the Mayor, who stopped dumbfounded; at his heels, Pascal in sandals, Théophile in his celluloid collar, and Jean de Jacques, looking more rapscallion than ever in his crumpled felt hat. "Bah!" said Pascal, shaking hands and anxious to excuse himself, "there's no hurry about *your* job. One day's as good as another and hail's just a joke for you." The Superintendent of Roads tried to turn some elegant phrase, but the mauve rosette of the Engineer left him too petrified—that rosette which a cruel destiny still denied him for three or four years to come.

When they had all drunk, sat down, cleared their throats, and the surly Secretary had opened wide his impressive portfolio, the Engineer crushed out his cigar, pushed away the wineglasses, and resumed his official rôle. Leaning his little plump hands on the table, with unctuous solemnity, he began: "Messieurs!" Théophile gave a nod of approval. "I am commissioned to liquidate with you, *once for all*, the question of the electric lighting of Mont-Paon—to cancel all schemes altogether, or—let's have no mistake about this—to put the work straight in hand. No more shilly-shallying. Is it yes, or no?"

"Eh?—as a matter of fact—" began the Mayor, mumbling his words, "as a matter of fact, it's *neither* yes *nor* no —it would perhaps be advisable..."

"You *must* make up your minds, Monsieur le Maire. It's high time!"

"Yes, yes," broke in Théophile. "No more delays, no more empty phrases, no more evasions. Action's what we want!"

"Hear, hear!" from Pascal.

"And the money?" growled Jean de Jacques.

Then the Reactionaries and the Party of Progress began to bandy frantically to and fro the ruinous cost of copper wire, that alarming loan, the horror of those extra centimes on the rates, the pennilessness of the countryside, the blessings of Civilization, the interests of the rural population, honour, precedent, the right of everybody to due illumination...

"No, no, the money first!"

"No, no, we've had vexations enough!"

"You're pouring cold water on the whole spirit of enterprise."

"You just want to clean us out!"

"Time we countryfolk stopped being a joke!"

"No debts for *us*!"

"Light for everyone!"

"No, justice!—for once!"

"Are we to go on being mere outcasts, pariahs, stick-in-the-muds?"

"And bumpkins?"

"We shall always be beggars," concluded Jean de Jacques, amid the uproar. "That's the long and short of it, my good man—beggars!"

Then the Engineer (who was decidedly warming to his rôle) planted his elbows on the table and called his hearers to order with lifted hand and a look of gravity—"You are only poor, Messieurs," said he, "because you *choose* to be! I mean it!"

"Hear, hear!" cried Pascal enthusiastically.

"The devil we are!" said the Mayor, scratching his ear.

"And the whole thing can be arranged for you..."

"Without paying?"

"Without paying. On *one* condition..."

The Superintendent of Roads felt his spirits rise; Jean de Jacques gave a sardonic grin; the Mayor drew his chair closer.

"Let us rule out of account," began the Engineer in casual tones, "all State-subsidies! Even supposing the State and the Département allowed you, at the highest, say, two-thirds of this expense, where are you going to raise the fifty thousand francs remaining as your share?"

"Not out of my pocket, I promise you," cried the Mayor with emphasis.

"Nor from our ordinary Budget," added the crumpled felt hat.

"That's precisely my point. Accordingly, the method I propose—the only one—is this. Pass a resolution to the effect that (as is obvious to anybody) your commune of a hundred and twenty inhabitants has absolutely no justification for its existence; that your finances will not suffice in future to pay for the most elementary conveniences; and petition unanimously" (all heads spontaneously recoiled)—"I repeat, unanimously, for the abolition pure and simple of your Mairie and your absorption in Arles."

Beneath such a blow our Superintendent of Roads flushed crimson. The first man in his village for thirty years, was he to end by sinking to be "the second at Rome"? "Schch..." whispered Pascal. The Mayor averted his eyes.

Swept away by the flood of his own eloquence, the Engineer had never noticed these dumb emotions in his hearers. His dazzled vision was busy contemplating his own rain of gold. "Then they'll attach you to your wealthy neighbour Arles. They'll electrify your countryside. They'll build you a station, a post-office, a washing-place, a cemetery. They'll install telephones. They'll assign you a resident medical officer. They'll open you a co-operative grocery. The Arlesians will foot the bill for all your expenditure, and you'll have all the advantages, without the slightest trouble..."

The Mayor pushed over his cap from one ear to the other: "My good Sir, the pace you go at...!"

"But consider that with the cost of living six times..."

If our Mayor was considering anything at that moment, it was certainly not (one could have sworn from the way he was nodding his head) our miserable cost of living.

"Yes," he said at last, "it's quite true, we *are* poor at Mont-Paon; but we prefer, we do, to manage our own affairs."

"The fact remains, my dear sir, that, as things are, without a sou there's not much you *can* manage! The progressive section of your Council will be the first to recognize..."

Then Théophile rose. With a roll of thunder outside in the darkening sky, his hour at last was come. Sticking out his thin chest, with forefinger thrust beneath the decorated collar of his coat (a gesture acquired since his achievement of that violet ribbon), he majestically delivered his verdict: "The Party of Progress makes me its mouthpiece to inform you, Monsieur l'Ingénieur, that this commune has always been free; and free, in spite of all, it proposes to remain."

The Engineer gnawed his lip to contain his laughter— "But, I say, look here—"

"Pardon me," interrupted Théophile. "Just two words, by your leave—to prevent any misunderstanding. From time immemorial—to be exact, since the year One (our registers will bear me out)—we have been a commune. They may take it as they will in higher circles: but while I remain a member of this Council and my voice carries any weight upon it, we will remain our own masters! What would our children say...?"

"Hear, hear!" applauded Pascal yet again. "What *would* our children say...? We must remain our own masters."

The Engineer could no longer control his laughter. "Your own masters?—but how? Free?—to do what?"

"Ah, Monsieur," exclaimed the Mayor, in heart-felt tones, "if *you* had held the reins like us for over thirty years, you would find that when the time came to hand them over..."

"Well," laughed the plump Engineer, "your children, if you'll allow me to say so, will have good grounds for saying, if they have neither light nor washing-place nor—"

"Yes. But Liberty, at all costs!—that indefeasible right..." intoned Théophile, with the emphasis appropriate to a journalist who has been decorated with the Palm. "For I hold, Monsieur, that the peoples are free..."

Unfortunately the surly Secretary had little love for rhetoric, journalese, civil liberty, or even, it may be, for Palms. "If you have no objection," said he with bitter curtness, snapping up his portfolio, "be as free as you please, but pay us—now, at all events—for our plans! You've had our bill for them a pretty time; and so far as I can see..." An explosion of croaking laughter at his back made him start violently. It was Jean de Jacques, his mind now set at rest about the electric lamps; Jean still master of his freedom, and as worthy of it as his sans-

culotte fathers before him, bidding us all good night—
resolved to be home in time, even on this cloudy evening,
to go to bed without a candle.

★   ★   ★

Hence it is that, down to the year '40 (as the archives
will bear witness), you are, my brothers of Mont-Paon,
condemned to your old ways and your ancient liberty.
That heavy official portfolio has closed upon and shat-
tered the four pallid electric lamps that should have
starred our tranquil nights. The surveyor's plan, in black
ink and azure on its earth-coloured ground, has reached
by now a ripe old age. But no hand will transfix the
iridescent neck of our Peacock with the treacherous arrow
of Progress. Light your lamps, dear Mont-Paonnais, buy
yourselves lanterns or, if you prefer, go to bed with the
sun; but sleep on in peace, my friends. Arles, your opulent
neighbour, is in no danger of annexing you. No one will
ask you, now, to sell your honour for washing-place or
telephone, cemetery or clock! What matter? Your
brooks still run in sparkling zig-zags at your housewives'
service. You still read in Heaven the time of day. And
every day, too, your train whistles it. Forgotten by the
P.L.M., you will preserve untouched, on this charming
branch-line ignored by the great world, your reed-built
Halt where the hornets nest. Not a station-lamp, not a
ticket-barrier, not a level-crossing gate! But, when
Hilarion shall have retired, and Pascal grown old in his
winter-quarters by the fire, your children bent on revelry
will manage just as well, in their turn, to kindle an auto-

da-fé of newspapers upon the track to make "the Crawler" carry them, willy-nilly, to the *Folies* of Arles!

Thanks to the sturdy independence of your Progressive
Party, you are condemned, I am afraid, to remain "Back-
woodsmen." But what of it? As members for life of
your Council, you will at least all meet again on winter
evenings to hold your fraternal gatherings in that pastoral
Mairie where are debated, instead of the communal
finances, the swellings of rabbits and the black blight on
olives. For long years yet, under the sardonic eye of the
Republic, gaily enthroned above all her warring factions,
Caruso shall sing to us the graces of Naples, and we will
empty "To Friendship" those bottles of mountain-wine
that mellow in your prison.

For, together with your ill-inked stamp, emblem of
your independence; with your frisking remounts, your
Bonapartist-minded Drainage Board, your moth-eaten
flag, green now with old age; with your fantastic
Records and your Budgets more dried up than your
brooks in August, you will keep, dear friends—dear
sunlit land, in your tranquillity you too will keep—the
imperturbable Liffran smiling at his flock; Zène with
those wrinkles of his that smile at everything; Théophile,
the great exorcist; your Mayor, "letting the world wag
and finding all's well that end's well"; and your Mayor's
Secretary, shamelessly marooned by the Prefect at Mont-
Paon, on the engaging salary of three hundred francs
a year.

For EU product safety concerns, contact us at Calle de José Abascal, 56–1°, 28003 Madrid, Spain or eugpsr@cambridge.org.

www.ingramcontent.com/pod-product-compliance
Ingram Content Group UK Ltd.
Pitfield, Milton Keynes, MK11 3LW, UK
UKHW020316140625
459647UK00018B/1895